CREDIT REPAIR

Mandatory Steps to Know in Order to Repair Your Credit Score

(The Ultimate Guide to Fast Credit Repair)

Leonard Curry

Published by Knowledge Icons

Leonard Curry

All Rights Reserved

*Credit Repair: Mandatory Steps to Know in Order to Repair
Your Credit Score (The Ultimate Guide to Fast Credit Repair)*

ISBN 978-1-990084-78-2

Legal & Disclaimer

The information contained in this book is not designed to replace or take the place of any form of medicine or professional medical advice. The information in this book has been provided for educational and entertainment purposes only.

The information contained in this book has been compiled from sources deemed reliable, and it is accurate to the best of the Author's knowledge; however, the Author cannot guarantee its accuracy and validity and cannot be held liable for any errors or omissions. Changes are periodically made to this book. You must consult your doctor or get professional medical advice before using any of the suggested remedies, techniques, or information in this book.

TABLE OF CONTENTS

Introduction

This book will be your complete road map for everything related to the art of growing, maintaining, and fixing a credit score. It's no secret that financial terms and processes can serve to be a bit tricky and murky for the average consumer. Sometimes it can even seem like a banking institution intentionally confuses its customers by mailing out notices that are filled with confusing financial verbiage and promises that always end up having a catch. This book will not only define some of these complicated terms, but will also provide priceless tips on how to avoid the tricks that banks use to trap their customers. By becoming more knowledgeable about what these terms mean and through the explanation of other ways in which a credit score can be improved over time, you'll be well on your way to borrowing money for that boat you always wanted in no time.

This book contains proven steps and strategies on how to become a truly smart consumer. In today's consumption-driven world, paying for a purchase with a credit card has become the easiest way in which to make a transaction. What most people don't think about as they slide their card (or insert their chip) into the card reader is that the frequency and way in which they pay back these bank credit lenders can affect other aspects of their life. A credit score can be described as the equivalent to proving to lending businesses that you are going to be able to pay them back within a reliable time frame. A credit score can also be beneficial when people like landlords and car dealerships want to make sure that you're responsible with your payment plans. Knowing the steps to take to repair and maintain a credit score is simply an essential when buying goods in today's economy.

Here's an inescapable fact: you will need to develop good spending habits, have an easy-to-follow plan at your disposal and be able to recognize when you are spending beyond your means in order to repair and maintain a respectable credit score. The contents of this book will give you a plan to follow and tips on how to recognize when you might be spending more than you should be, but the ability to develop good spending habits is a skill that will take more than the information presented in this book. After learning what it takes to develop good spending habits, it will be up to you as a savvy consumer to practice these techniques in real life. While the information presented in this book will be beneficial to you, practical implementation will be the only true way for you to become well versed in the techniques presented. It's important to remember that a crucial aspect of experience is making mistakes. Throughout the process of learning to fix your credit, don't be too hard on yourself. Of course, the goal of any credit fix is not to make more mistakes in order to progress towards a good credit score, but learning is part of the process. There are always resources that can help you beyond the scope of this book, which we will discuss in subsequent chapters.

Chapter 1: Budgeting Your Money, The Easy Way

If you're looking to get out of debt the most important thing you need to do is make sure you know where your money is going. You want to make sure that you understand how much you owe to each place, company or person and then you'll be able to take the time and make the effort to actually create a budget that works.

For many people, the very idea of creating a budget is daunting. How can you possibly figure out how much money you should send to everyone when you don't even really know how much money you have or how much money you owe or which one you should pay off first? There's just too many questions involved and you find yourself completely thrown off and confused.

That's why step one is making sure you know how much you owe and to whom.

Start by making a list of all the information you have. List the amount of money that's owed, who you owe it to and whether the amount is currently a collection or is just 'past due.' Both of these categories are important but knowing the difference will help you understand which to pay off first.

Past due accounts are those that you owe to a credit company but they are still contacting you asking for payment. They haven't revoked your credit yet, they're just tacking on a lot of fines, fees and interest for as long as you don't pay the account. These accounts are going to look back on your credit report (which we'll talk about later) but they aren't going to be as bad as collection accounts. These types of accounts are generally capable of being paid off in monthly payments (regular credit card payments)

A collection account is one where the credit company has completely given up on getting their money back. What they do is they sell the debt to a collection agencies and that agency attempts to get the money back from you. This is money that has been overdue for a long period of time and you know owe the entire amount is due all at the same time. In some instances you can get the company to take payments or accept a lower settlement but you're generally responsible for the entire account.

When you're working on creating a budget you want to make sure you're paying at least a little bit of money on each of your past due accounts because this encourages them to keep the account open. They want to get as much money from you as possible and if they choose to close the account and turn it into a collection that won't happen. So they keep the account open as long as you continue to pay (even if you aren't making full monthly payments and the fees are still racking up.

With a collection you need to contact the company if you want to attempt to make payments (usually not easy) or you need to pay off the entire amount (or settlement amount) all at the same time. This means you need to come up with all the money or you really can't do anything about the account.

When you create your budget you want to think about everything that you have coming into the home and then think about every bill that you have. The bills that are considered current you want to keep current. These are helping your credit score even as other past due bills are hurting it. These are bills like your lights, electricity, water and food. Make sure you have enough money set aside monthly to pay for all of these things. Determine how much money you need in order to pay off those current bills and then look at what's left over. A portion of this should go into a savings account. Try to get at least $50 to go to savings every month. This will help you slowly build up a little nest egg in case of emergencies.

The money that's left over needs to be divided over the rest of your past due bills. Try to at least reach the minimum payment amount on your credit cards or accounts that are considered past due. This will help you keep from getting additional fees for not meeting the minimum payment amount. If you can afford to pay the amount that's past due you'll be even better off but try to keep the account open. That means you want to keep some type of charge on the account so they don't close it.

If you're past due on an account it's more likely that they will close the account once they get your money. As we'll talk about in a later chapter, this isn't something that you want to happen. That means you want to keep a balance on the card but try to keep it current instead of past due. This will help you build your credit back up.

Once you've taken the minimum payment amount for each of your past due accounts try to see what's left. If there's anything left see if it will come close to the payoff amount for one of your collection accounts. If it's close you may be able to negotiate with the company (which we'll discuss in our chapter about collection agencies).

Your budget should go somewhere that you can see it easily and often. You don't want to mess up your budget because that's going to keep you on track with your spending and with paying off bills. That will get you out of debt faster and help you get back to having fun with your money (instead of giving it to everyone else for nothing).

Chapter 2: Whyyour Credit Score Matters

In recent years, a simple three-digit number has become critical to your financial life. This number, known as a credit score, is designed to predict the possibility that you won't pay your bills. Credit scores are handy for lenders, but they can have enormous repercussions for your wallet, your future, and your peace of mind.

Your FICO or credit score is an overall evaluation of your financial health that helps lenders determine your creditworthiness. Credit scores affect whether you can get credit and what you pay for credit cards, auto loans, mortgages and other types of credit. Higher credit scores mean you are more likely to be approved for most kinds of credit and pay a lower interest rate for that credit.

Your credit score can come between you and many things in life. Since a FICO score is the excepted standard for many companies, a low score will mean you have to pay higher interest rates, if you can get a loan at all. It can also mean that you will have to pay higher deposits for utilities such as telephone, electricity, cellular phone plans and many other services. While this may not seem fair to most consumers, it is done by companies to determine whether or not they can rely on you to pay your bills on time.

Typically, those with a lower credit score have issues with paying their debts or paying them on time. This indicates to companies and banks that the person is probably a high-risk case and if they do decide to approve the loan or service, they must protect themselves from that risk by charging more. It is an excepted practice that can restrict or impede the lives of many people.

Your credit score is a valuable asset for many reasons. A very good score allows you to obtain credit more easily and at lower interest rates. But a high credit score can also help you qualify for a cell phone, avoid or reduce a deposit paid for utilities for your home or apartment, and get lower insurance premiums. Your credit score may also be used by potential employers and landlords as a screening tool. Your credit score is very valuable, and you should treat it like the asset it is and always work on improving it.

Three-quarters of all lenders use FICO scores when considering requests for loans or credit. To enhance your chances of being approved for any type of credit and get the best interest rates, your score should be 720 or higher.

Lenders look at your credit scores all the time. They look at your scores when deciding, for example, to extend credit to you, or whether to change your interest rate or credit limit on an existing credit card or to send you an offer through the mail. Having good credit scores makes your financial transactions much easier and can save you money on lower interest rates, lower insurance premiums, and reduced deposits or down payments.

That's why your credit score is a vital part of your financial health.

How Your Credit Score Affects You

If your credit score is high enough, you'll qualify for a lender's best rates and terms. Your mailbox will be stuffed with low-rate offers from credit card issuers, and mortgage lenders will fight for your business. You'll get great deals on auto financing if you need a car, home loans if you want to buy or improve a house, and small business loans if you decide to start a new venture. If your score is low or nonexistent, however, you'll enter a no-man's land where mainstream credit is all but impossible to come by. If you find someone to lend you money, you'll pay high rates and fat fees for the privilege. A bad or even mediocre credit score can easily cost you tens of thousands and even hundreds of thousands of dollars in your lifetime. You don't even have to have tons of credit problems to pay a price. Sometimes all it takes is a single missed payment to knock more than 100 points off your credit score and put you in a lender's high-risk category. That would be scary enough if we were just talking about loans. But landlords and insurance companies also use credit scores to evaluate applicants. A good score can win you cheaper premiums and better apartments; a bad score can make insurance more expensive and a place to live hard to find.

Yet too many people know far too little about credit scores and how they work. Here's just a sample of the kinds of emails and letters I get every day from people puzzling over their credit:

"I just closed all of my credit card accounts trying to improve my credit.

Now I hear that closing accounts can actually hurt my score. How can I recover from this? Should I try to reopen accounts so that I can have a higher amount of available credit?" Hallie in Shreveport, LA"

I joined a credit-counseling program because I was in way over my head. But my wife and I plan on buying a house within the next three

years, and she has expressed concern that my participation in this debt management program could hurt my credit score. What should I do to help my overall chances with the mortgage process and get the best rate possible?" Paul in Lodi, NJ

What these readers sense, and what credit experts know, is that ignorance about your credit score can cost you. Sometimes people with great scores get offered lousy loan deals but don't realize they can qualify for better terms. More often, people with bad or mediocre credit get approved for loans but don't realize the high price they're paying.

What It Costs Long Term to Have a Poor or Mediocre Credit Score If you need an example of exactly how much a credit score can matter, let's examine how these numbers affect two friends, Emily and Karen. Both women got their first credit card in college and carried an $8,000 balance on average over the years. (Carrying a balance isn't smart financially, but unfortunately, it's an ingrained habit with many credit card users.) Emily and Karen also bought new cars after graduation, financing their purchases with $20,000 auto loans. Every seven years, they replaced their existing cars with new ones until they bought their last vehicles at age 70. Each brought her first home with $350,000 mortgages at age 30 and then moved up to a larger house with $450,000 mortgages after turning 40.

Neither has ever suffered the embarrassment of being rejected for a loan or turned down for a credit card. But here the similarities end. Emily was always careful to pay her bills on time, all the time, and typically paid more than the minimum balance owed. Lenders responded to her responsible use of credit by offering her more credit cards at good rates and terms. They also tended to increase her credit limits regularly. That allowed Emily to spread her credit card balance across several cards. All these factors helped give Emily an excellent credit score. Whenever a lender tried to raise her interest rate, she would politely threaten to transfer her balance to another card. As a result, Emily's average interest rate on her cards was 9.9 percent. Karen, by contrast, didn't always pay on time, frequently paid only the minimum due and tended to max out the cards that she had. That made lenders reluctant to increase her credit limits or offer her new cards. Although the two women owed the same amount on average, Karen tended to carry larger balances on fewer cards. All these factors hurt Karen's credit—not enough to prevent her from getting loans, but enough for lenders to charge her more. Karen had much less negotiating power when it came to interest rates. Her average interest rate on her credit cards was 19.9 percent.

Emily's careful credit use paid off with her first car loan. She got the best available rate, and she continued to do so every time she bought a new car until her last purchase at age 70. Thanks to her lower credit score, Karen's rate was three percentage points higher.

Karen's total lifetime penalty for less-than-stellar credit? More than $190,000.

If anything, these examples underestimate the true financial cost of mediocre credit:

• The interest rates in the examples are relatively low in historical terms. Higher prevailing interest rates would increase the penalty that Karen pays.

• Karen probably paid insurance premiums that were 20 percent to 30 percent higher than Emily's and she might have had more trouble finding an apartment, all because of her credit.

• The examples don't count "opportunity cost"—what Karen could have achieved financially if she weren't paying so much more interest.

Because more of Karen's paycheck went to lenders, she had less money available for other goals: vacations, a second home, college educations for her kids, and retirement. In fact, if Karen had been able to invest the extra money she paid in interest instead of sending it to banks and credit card companies, her savings might have grown by a whopping $2 million by the time she was 70. With so much less disposable income and financial security, you wouldn't be surprised if Karen also experienced more anxiety about money. Financial problems can take their toll in innumerable ways, from stress-related illnesses to marital problems and divorce.

Chapter 3: What You Need To Know

About Credit Scores

So before we start discussing how to improve your credit score, we should first discuss what it is and why you need to do that.

Basically, a credit score is a number that has three digits, which is produced by credit scoring agencies using a certain mathematical formula that incorporates many different kinds of financial information that can be found in your credit report. Credit scores are designed with one thing in mind: To determine or estimate your chances of becoming substantially delinquent or unable to pay off your credit obligations within the next 24 months. This is also known as credit risk.

Today, there are several credit scoring models that are being used by top credit scoring agencies all over the world. One of the most important, if not the most important, credit scoring models is the FICO credit score. According to the organization's website, it is estimated that up to 90% of financial services organizations in the United States utilize credit scores generated by FICO in deciding whether or not to grant credit to applicants.

All credit scores, whether it's from FICO or the others, indicate your level of credit risk, i.e., your chances of becoming delinquent in paying off your financial obligations in the next 24 months. The way they work is that the higher your credit score is, the lower your credit risk is and vice versa. So when you talk about improving your credit score, you're talking about increasing it.

Components of a Credit Score

For general discussion purposes, we will consider FICO as our credit score reference. This is because as mentioned earlier, FICO is the single biggest credit rating agency because up to 90% of all financial institutions in the United States use their scores for their credit-granting decisions. Anyway, all credit rating agencies typically consider the same major areas for computing your credit score so using FICO as reference is a logical approach for our discussions.

The five major components of FICO's credit scoring system are your payment history, the amount you owe, your credit history's average age, kinds of credit you have available at your disposal, attempts to obtain new credit accommodations, and other demographic or personal types of information. Payment history accounts for about 35% of your total FICO credit score and includes details such as delinquent payments – if any – and records that are made public pertaining to your financial obligations. The amount of money you owe comprises 30% of total credit score and in particular, the amount of owed money classified as revolving has heavier weight in this particular component.

The average age of your credit history accounts for 15% of your FICO credit score and takes into consideration the date and number of years from when you first borrowed money from financial institutions. The kind of credit facilities you've availed of since the beginning and until now accounts for about 10% of your total FICO score, and also takes into consideration the ratio of revolving and installment credit to total amounts owed. Attempts to obtain new credit accommodations – or new credit – comprise another 10% of your total FICO credit score and refers to actions like the number of accounts recently opened and even the number of inquiries you have made with different financial institutions.

The Effect of Your Financial Mistakes on Your Credit Score

In general, the financial booboos you've committed over the years can have numerous effects – the degrees of which vary – on your credit scores, depending on the model used or the credit scoring agency that issues your credit score. While it's true that all of them generally use the same types of information when it comes to generating credit scores, what is different among them is the weight assigned to each of the components or types of information. That's why financial blunders can have varying effects or degrees of effects on credit scores across different credit scores.

Each credit-scoring methodology or model uses several formulas in order to arrive at a final score or rating. Each of the formulas being used by different agencies was created for use with specific types or groups of borrowers. So which formula is being used to determine your credit score? The information contained in your credit report is what determines the type of credit-scoring methodology or formula that'll be used.

If you're a rookie borrower, i.e., someone who has just borrowed money for the first time, then you would be grouped along with other borrowers who have relatively young credit histories too, and the credit scoring agency computing your credit score will use a specific algorithm or formula to determine the credit scores of people in your group or bracket.

The Good Thing about Credit Scores

If you're very responsible when it comes to the use of credit facilities, then don't be surprised to find that your credit score will be high, which will provide you with several key benefits. The first of such benefits is the ability to easily borrow money when you need it and at lower interest rate to boot. Because a high credit score means low credit risk, financial institutions will be willing to lend you money at lower interest compared to those who have lower credit scores. For instance, an auto loan of $25,000 at 6.5% interest, over a 5 year period, including fees down payment, would cost in total, about $30,529.38. However, if you follow the steps in this book, achieve a good credit score, if you reduced your annual interest by 2%, if not more, then that same loan would cost about $29,421.62, a $1,107.38 difference! That is another vacation, just by having good credit score.

The second benefit to having good credit score is the ease of getting approved when you apply for a utilities account such as cable, Internet, mobile phone, and water. Again, the point being here is that a high score means low credit risk. If your credit risk is low, then utility companies know the chances of you skipping on payments can be very low and as such, they can quickly approve your applications. A common problem for many college students, is that after they graduate college at the age of 22, they go to apply for an apartment, and get denied due to having bad, or no credit at all.

Lastly, it may be much easier for you to find a job if you have a very good credit score. Why? If you have low credit risk, it means your finances are generally in order. If that's the case, then your risk for being tempted to steal from companies or easily quit as soon as a higher paying job becomes available may be significantly lower than those whose financial situations are in shambles.

The opposites can be true if your credit scores are low. With higher credit risks, you'll have a harder time obtaining new credit, getting approved for utilities, and finding a new job.

Chapter 4: Understanding Your Credit

Score

In this chapter, we will go through some basics so that you understand what lies at the core of your credit report, your credit score, and how it affects you. Your credit score can be seen as an amalgamation of all of your credit history – you get points for doing things right, like paying your bills on time, and have points deducted when you do things wrong, like paying less than the minimum installment.

In this instance, I will go through the FICO scoring system we use in the U.S. so that you can see exactly what constitutes a good score and bad one.

What is a Bad Credit Score?

In this case, you want the highest score possible. If your score is 619 or less, you are considered a bad credit risk and are unlikely to be able to access any form of financing. A score this low indicates someone that has arrears in terms of their bills is a constant bad payer or maybe even someone with debt that is in collection.

What is the Average Score?

The average American has a score of around 692 and this is considered a fair score.

If you score is between 620 and 699, you are considered a fair risk and, while you may be able to get financing, you are going to have to pay for that privilege. Scores that fall within this range are still considered low and higher risk when it comes to lending.

What is a Good Score?

If you have a fico score of between 700 and 749, you have a good rating.

If you fall into this category, you will find it easier to get credit as this score generally indicates that you are a responsible lender and are reasonably good at keeping your accounts up to date. This indicates that you never allow your bills to become more than 30 days overdue.

What may surprise you is that you still won't have access to the very best interest rates that the company has to offer. These are reserved for those with excellent credit.

What is an Excellent Score?

To fall into this category, you need to have a credit rating of 750 – 850. If you do fall in this category, you have proven that you manage your debt responsibly, always pay on time and seldom, if ever, max out your cards. This is what most credit providers would classify as the perfect borrower and the rates that are offered will reflect that.

It is the classic conundrum – you can really only get a great deal on credit if you can prove that you do not need credit.

Is your Fico Score Fixed?

Fortunately, if you have a bad credit rating, your FICO score is not some immutable number – you can actually work at improving it by modifying your actions over time. As long as you are consistent in your attempts, you will be able to get your FICO score to increase.

The truth is that it is simple to work the system so that your score improves. It can be something as simple as waiting a week or so after paying your credit card before using it again, or even just bumping up the amount you pay every month.

And you can monitor the progress so you can see what is working and what is not. What is also great is that whilst these steps may not drastically improve your FICO score immediately, the companies who monitor these things will be able to see that your overall behavior in terms of your debt has changed – they will see that you are becoming a more responsible borrower and that you are better able to manage the debt that you have. This can be a big positive for you.

Chapter 5: Why Is Credit Important?

You may not realize it but your credit score is actually extremely important to your entire life. If you have bad credit you are going to pay more for just about everything that you buy. That's because everyone who gives you credit examines the score you have. They use that score to understand what is the risk that you will not pay the money that they lend you. In order to mitigate their risk they will increase your interest rate so that you pay more each month. That way, if in the end you default on the money, they've already made more from you.

Look at it this way. Your credit is generally measured on a scale from 0 up to 800 (there are other scales but we'll stick with the general ones for now). If your score is 0 it means you don't have credit and that's bad. It doesn't look good when companies look to figure out if you deserve credit. It can be difficult to get that first card.

What's even worse is if you have credit but it's bad credit. This is when you're in the 500 range or even the 600's. (Anything lower and you are really in trouble.) If you have a score in the 500's or lower you are a high risk to any company that gives you credit. That means if you are given credit you have a higher likelihood of never paying it back. Credit companies really don't like that idea.

If you have a low score and you go to a bank to apply for a loan you may end up with an interest rate of, let's say 2.5%. Given how high interest rates are you'll probably just shrug and say 'well that's just how the economy is.' But what if we told you your neighbor has a 700 credit score and they just got the same loan for 1.5% interest? You wouldn't like that so much right? Well that's the kind of thing that can happen if you don't have a good credit score. You pay more on interest for your loans.

Unfortunately, you actually pay higher interest on everything from car loans, mortgages, and student loans to credit cards and everything in between. So what that means is you are actually paying more money just to go through life than someone else would. Plus you have a lower chance of actually being approved for any of these things because your credit score is low. A low credit score affects you in any area of your life that gives you credit. So that means any and all credit cards, credit accounts (loans and such) and even housing.

Yes even housing will consider your credit score, especially if you're looking at townhouses, apartments or anything that has a monthly fee associated with it. That's because the owner wants to make sure that they can count on you to pay your bills every month when they come due. If you haven't paid other people (as evidenced by your low credit score) they assume that you also aren't going to pay them. In some instances they may require a larger security deposit or an extra month's rent to hold in escrow before they rent to you. In other cases they may refuse to grant you housing at all.

By improving your credit score you can cut down on all of these things. You can improve the way that you live because you'll be able to get the nicer apartment, a nicer car, a better house and even a credit card with a low interest rate. You'll be able to live your life the way you want instead of having to spend all of your money on that interest payment. It's definitely going to be worth it and it's going to help your

family in more ways than even we can tell
you.

The problem is getting your credit where you want it to be. Now if you already have bad credit you know how it happened. You know that you've done a few things wrong but you really want to make some changes and start getting everything back in order. Luckily for you it's actually a lot easier than you might think to start building your credit back up. You're going to have to spend some time and expend some effort but at the same time you're going to have to be patient. Your credit score won't improve overnight.

One thing to keep in mind is that the entire process should be a family affair. Keep in mind that if you have a partner living in the home with you their score is going to be important as well. That means if you have bad credit and you share any purchases (like your house or car) that's going to affect them as well. The opposite is also true so if you get your credit looking great but they don't you may still have trouble getting credit when you want it in the future. Make sure you talk with them about making some changes as well.

Chapter 6: Get A Copy Of Your Credit Report

" I just knew I had bad credit so I was afraid to even look at it for a very long time. When I finally worked up the courage to see it, I was not very surprised however there were several things on my report that were mistakes and shouldn't have been there."

I know it can be scary and even nauseating to think of all the bad monsters on your credit report, but more often than not, it's not as bad as it seems. Trust me, you want to know exactly what is on your report and remember, admitting the problem is the very first step to recovery.J Looking at your credit report will tell you exactly what you should be focusing on that is pulling down your credit score.

Random Fact: According to the FACT Act or, federal Fair and Accurate Credit Transactions Act, every U.S. resident is eligible to receive one free credit report every 12 months from each of the major credit reporting companies. To learn more, please visit the FACT Act website at: www.annualcreditreport.com.

After you get your credit report, look it over very closely and the first things you want to check for are mistakes, errors, or even fraudulent claims that will require disputing. The average number of U.S. identity fraud victims annually is 11,571,900, so it would behoove you to make sure that you catch something like this on your report as soon as possible. It happens frequently to many people, I myself included, and unless you constantly have updated information about what exactly is on your credit report, you may fall victim to this and have no awareness of it until you go to apply for credit, whether it be buying a car or moving into your brand new home, and be completely caught off-guard. Checking your credit report regularly can prevent situations like from happening thus making the experience of buying a car, home, or paying off bad debt all the more pleasant. We all know bad things happen but you can prevent certain occurrences from sitting too long, and having devastating impacts on your credit score. There are even certain programs and services out there that will alert you when your identity has been jeopardized. I am not sure on which company is best but an internet search and a little research could answer your various questions. After going through your credit report and checking for fraudulent activity you then must check for faults or errors that may appear and in this case you must contact the particular company and dispute a claim.

There are several ways to dispute a claim and anything faulty should be addressed as soon as possible. One way is by calling the lender to make sure that the information they have is accurate. After, if there is still an issue, you will have to continue with filing the dispute. You will have to find the all information from your credit report and either write the company a letter or submit a form (which I will provide at the end of the book), and send it to them. Make sure to always keep a record by either making a copy of the letter or if doing online, by printing a copy of the form you are submitting. You are going to be asking them to have the error removed from your credit report and providing any proof you have that the mistake is on their part and not on you. After this process, when you have carefully gone over your credit report and removed errors or realizing that there are none, start looking at the balances with either the highest interest rates or those with balances above the 30 percent, or, the credit utilization ration.

-Credit Utilization Ratio

In case you were wondering, the credit utilization ratio compares the amount that is being spent versus the total amount available to the borrower. The credit utilization ratio is but one of several ways that a credit score is calculated. So, if you have a high credit limit and very little debt, then you are doing well and this will benefit your credit score. Experts say that you should keep your debt to lower than 30% of the total available amount, which is also known as the credit-to-debt ratio. If there are cards where you owe more than 30% of the balance, make sure to pay those down to the smallest amount possible as soon as you are able to which brings me to the next step of comparing all of your credit limits.

Where Can You Get Your Credit Report and Score for Free?

You can get your credit report from each of the three major reporting agencies— Equifax, Experian, and TransUnion—for free once a year at annualcreditreport.com. But credit reports don't include your actual credit score— you usually have to pay for those. However, I recently joined Credit Karma, at creditkarma.com, where you can actually get it for free

Chapter 7: Your Money Blueprint

Our money blueprint guides our spending habits. It is our mindset about money; our deeply held beliefs about the way money should be treated. Our money blueprint was instilled in us during childhood, and comes from our parents' beliefs about money. As a result we are conditioned to behave either negatively or positively with money. If we grew up in a frugal household we be more frugal. If we grew up in a wasteful household we might be more likely to spend frivolously.

"Money doesn't grow on trees."

"Don't spend money you don't have."

"Money can't buy happiness."

These are phrases many of us heard growing up, and whether we know it or not, they have affected our feelings about money into adulthood. Because of this many of us are already pre-programmed either struggle or prosper financially. If we grew up in a frugal household we may be more frugal.

Although our money blueprint is deeply entrenched in our subconscious, it is possible to change our money mindset.

To rid ourselves of money issues and get on the right financial track once and for all, we have to reset our thinking.

Find Out Your Money Blueprint

Here is a brief and basic technique to help figure out your financial blueprint.

Take out a pencil and a sheet of paper. Start by asking yourself fundamental questions regarding money. Get a pencil and paper and jot down all of your feelings, thoughts and experiences as they pertain to money. Write down everything, even if they seem silly, embarrassing or weird.

Ask yourself:

1.   What are my beliefs about money?

Write down everything that comes to mind. Continue asking yourself this question until you've run out of answers. When you're done, move on to the next question.

2. What are my parents' beliefs about money? (Ask your parents.)

Write down everything that comes to mind. Continue asking yourself this question until you've run out of answers. When you're done, move on to the next question.

3. Who am I similar to when it comes to money? (Your money blueprint is probably similar to your parents. Were they savers or spenders? Were they avoiders? Did they manage money well or did they often mismanage? Were they investors? Did they educate you on how to deal with money? Are you repeating their money practices?)

Write down everything that comes to mind. Continue asking yourself this question until you've run out of answers. When you're done, move on to the next question

4. What are my spending and saving habits?

Write down everything that comes to mind. Continue asking yourself this question until you've run out of answers. When you're done, move on to the next question.

5. Did any events happen that molded my beliefs regarding money? Examples: eviction, running out of food, receiving a windfall like inheritance or winnings.

Write down everything that comes to mind. Continue asking yourself this question until you've run out of answers. When you're done, move on to the next question.

6.   Am I content to make just enough to get by, or is my goal to make hundreds, thousands, hundreds of thousands or millions of dollars?

Write down everything that comes to mind. Continue asking yourself this question until you've run out of answers. When you're done, move on to the next question.

7.   What are your values and priorities?

Place the following values in order of significance to you: Love, Health, Safety, Security, Honesty, Comfort, Money, Education, Integrity.

If money doesn't fall in your top three, it probably isn't a priority in your life. More than likely, you don't put enough time and energy into managing it.

When you've answered all of the questions go over your list. Combine two to three related answers into one, if possible. Next determine whether you feel each answer is negative or positive. Finally put a plus sign (+) after every answer you believe is an advantage toward achieving your financial goals, and a negative sign (-) after every point you believe is a disadvantage toward achieving your financial goals.

This record will be your MONEY BLUEPRINT on paper. All the negative points, are those that restrict your capability of obtaining financial freedom. The more negatives there are, the more limited are your abilities of becoming financially stable.

If you have more negatives than positives then you have to re-adjust your money blueprint. Until you do, you will continue to have difficulties with money. In order to do this, you have to change how you think about money.

It's a fact that rich people think differently about money and treat money differently than people who have little money. Another way to change our money blueprint is to begin to think the way they do.

Here are few ways rich people think act behave:

1.   Rich people don't overspend; they live below their means. If a purchase will put them farther from their financial goals, they forego the purchase. They don't take

out loans and go into debt to buy something they want. Instead, they think about money so they can make more to raise their means and make those extravagant purchases.

If you want to buy that car, that house, high-priced item, consider how it will affect your financial goals. If it's going to set you back instead of build you up, put it off, make more money then buy it when you can afford it.

2. Rich people think long-term. They plan for their financial futures and make decisions accordingly. When they make financial decisions they consider whether it will be beneficial or detrimental to their financial goals. They delay gratification in order to be wealthier tomorrow.

Again, if that expensive purchase is going to put a dent in your wallet or bank account, or increase your credit card debt, leave it alone until your account is healthy enough to withstand the blow.

3. Rich people teach their children to be rich and to know the value of a dollar. They prepare their children to handle a large amounts so that they understand that mishandling money can lead to it all being squandered away.

Early financial education is the best way to ensure your children don't develop an unhealthy relationship with money and spending. Children should learn to be rich, even if they don't come from a rich family.

4. Rich people take risks. They know that failure is always possible but they don't let

it keep them from making the decisions that may make them successful. If failure happens they pick themselves up and continue moving forward.

Fear of failure results in inaction. It's okay to take financial risks when the possibility of success is greater than the possibility of failure. Even if you fail, you can pick yourself up and keep going.

5. Rich people surround themselves with likeminded people. Successful people befriend other successful people. The same can be said for most people in almost every tax bracket.

If you want to elevate yourself financially, it's best to find other people who aspire to the same level of financial success. People who plan for success do better when they are around other people who plan for success.

Chapter 8: What Is Credit Score?

Credit simply means your ability to borrow. As such, your credit score is a numerical representation of the risk a lender faces if they were to lend money to you. It is based on the analysis of one's credit files/history. Another layman's definition is that it is the difference between being denied credit and being granted. Well, since money is often scarce, borrowing becomes a great option for sourcing funds to do whatever you want to do. It simply enables you to do things you would otherwise not afford if you were to be paying in cash. Credit score determines how lenders perceive you when advancing credit; when your score is high, it means you are a reliable borrower so you won't need to pay more but when the score is low, the lenders treat you with caution and charge you more to advance credit to you. The cost of borrowing (interest you pay) is usually linked to your credit score.

In other terms, the credit score determines how much you pay for mortgage, health insurance, car insurance, and lots of other things including your utilities, cell phones, car payments etc. Employers also look into credit scores lately before hiring, which means this can determine whether you are hired or not. As you can notice, if your score is not good, your life can be pretty much a nightmare. You probably will not even fathom the idea of living in your dream home, or driving your dream car because getting these will be literally out of reach. In simple terms, your credit score will ultimately determine the kind of lifestyle you live.

The Type of Data Used To Score Your Credit

Generally, there are five categories that constitute the FICO score.

*Payment history (35%): The potential lender wants to know whether you pay your credit accounts on time. Most lenders seem to be jittery about signs of late payments. They foresee default and delinquent encounters with such clients.

*Amounts owed (30%): Having accounts with balances doesn't necessarily mean that you are a bad borrower with low FICO scores. Most credit cards allow for minimum payments on your account as the balance revolves. If you have serviced your account effectively and promptly, you have little to worry about as far as your score is concerned.

*Longer credit history improves your score (15%): The rationale is that if you have been borrowing for a long time, then you are a good borrower, otherwise you would have been denied credit by those who considered your applications. There is a mistaken belief that avoiding credit is good for your credit score. This is misleading. Lenders need to know how you handle credit before they engage you. If you never handle credit, there is no telling what will happen; you might as well be a high risk. It is inadvertently construed to mean that you don't borrow because you can't pay.

However, it is possible to have a short credit history but still score high on FICO.

Some important factors that are taken into consideration include:

*The types of credit in use (10%): FICO also considers a combination of credit cards, installment loans, retail accounts and mortgage loans.

* New credit (10%)-The age of your accounts: the age of your oldest account and the age of your newest account is considered. They also take into account the average age of all accounts. Such information as how long it has been since you used the account is also assessed.

Note: Your personal and demographic information such as where you come from and your race or orientation (religious or social) does not affect your credit score. A high credit score allows you to access credit at a lower cost.

The Purpose of Credit Scores

Credit scores are designed to mitigate various types of risk. The most commonly mentioned risk is that of lending money to a borrower. It determines one's credit worthiness i.e. how lending money to you is risky. In other words, credit score is an objective way of measuring credit risk. It was introduced at a time when the process of granting credit was inconsistent, slow, and even unfairly biased. Here is a summary of why credit scoring is great.

#Credit scores allow people to get loans faster (almost instantly) since lenders can speed up the approval process. It is possible to make instant credit decisions if you are a lender, which means this helps borrowers, access credit fast.

#It is an objective way of making credit decisions: This focuses on facts than feelings which are unverifiable.

#There are few credit mistakes: The scoring puts into consideration many aspects thus making it fair in awarding credit even to people who have had a bad credit history

#There is more credit: Lenders approve more loans based on credit.

#Lower credit rates: There are more lenders (credit), which increases competition thus pushing the cost of credit lower.

The credit scores are availed in the credit report. There are many different models for scoring individual credit in the USA.

However, the most commonly used formula is the FICO score, which ranges from 300 to 850; the higher the rate, the better the credit and vice versa. There are three FICO scores as generated by the various credit reporting bureaus with the big three being: Experian, TransUnion and Equifax.

So, why should you keep your credit score high? Here are some reasons why you should keep your credit score as high as possible.

Why should your credit score be high?

- Cheaper credit: Lenders are more willing to offer a lower interest rate. Here is a practical scenario:

A credit score of 750 translates to a 6.11 interest on a 30 year $300,000 mortgage, while a credit score of 620 translates to a 7.42 interest on the same mortgage. As you can see, this difference will definitely translate into thousands of dollars over the 30-year mortgage period.

- It puts you on equal footing with creditors and lenders. You can comfortably negotiate knowing that lenders are competing to have you as their good risk borrower.

- In addition, businesses develop interest in your business because it is a high value asset courtesy of the low risk.

- Insurance companies also request for your credit report before deciding your premiums or even whether they will cover a risk for you.

Let me first explain how the credit system works just to make you understand where credit rating woes emanate and why it seems hard to keep your credit rating high.

Chapter 9: The Student Loan Debt Problem In The Us.

In the United States the cost of college education has been steadily increasing over the years, at the same time the value of education has also increased because of the belief many American have; that you need a college education to earn a higher salary. The belief that when a person has a college degree they are guaranteed a job and a higher salary have young Americans today taking on often times hefty debts to cover the costs to obtain a college education.

Students without a credit score or credit history are being approved for thousands of dollars in loans by lenders who are betting they'll be able to pay it back after getting a college degree. In order to meet those hefty debts, the students would need to find higher paying jobs that are not always available in this economic downturn the US have suffered since 2001.

The increasing cost of college.

In 1970, a University of Utah student would have spent about $390 a year on tuition cost. In 2012, that number has ballooned to $6,000 in tuition cost. This trend is not only limited to Utah. Across the country college tuition rates are skyrocketing. In 1976, college tuition cost was an average of $2,275 and by 2006 it shot up to $15,434 as an average cost for all college institutions. For public institutions the average cost of tuition was $1,789 in 1976 and went up to $11,034 in 2006. In 1976, the cost of tuition was $3,906 for private institutions and the tuition cost shot up to $28,384 by 2006. From 1982 to 2007, the national average increase at America's universities was 400 percent.

How the Federal government have caused the increase in the cost of college.

Financial aid and grants are supposed to make college more affordable and accessible for all students. The question that is coming to light is, what if by handing money out to undergrads, the government is simply encouraging schools to spend more and jack up tuition prices?

There is much debate over the reasons for the steep increase in college tuition. Many people believe the demand for higher education with the availability of federal funding and student loans has given colleges room to raise prices. For example many studies shows that for every extra dollar a college gets in Pell Grants, the school charges 40 cents more in the colleges tuition rate. For every extra dollar in subsidized student loans, tuition goes up 65 cents. The effects were much more pronounced at private colleges.

On the other side of the debate there are those who believe the decline in state funding for public education and the shrinking subsidies at private schools. The federal government has stepped up its lending accordingly, and so have private student lenders.

No matter what standpoint is correct, these debts lead to lots of problems for the students and the government or country as a whole. Very often students are not able to meet their debts leading to an increase in delinquency rates in the US. Studies show the delinquency rate on student loans is higher than credit cards, mortgages and auto loans which have all seen a decline in late payments. The total outstanding student loan balance is $1.08 trillion, and a whopping 11.5% of it is 90+ days delinquent or in default. That's the highest delinquency rate among all forms of debt and the only one that's been on the rise consistently since 2003.

How the debt will affect students in the next 10 years?

Student borrowers are delaying major life decisions, like buying a home or cars, because of credit issues as a result of their student loans. The rate of home ownership is 36% less among those currently repaying their student debt, according to research. The burden of student debt is limiting the ability of Americans to buy homes and start small businesses.

Student loans also affect Americans under this burden by causing them to postpone marriage and childbearing; do to the demand to pay student loan debt, the borrowers are many times force to follow different career paths. The need to repay loans is steering some away from professions like social work, health care and early childhood education toward higher-paying jobs in tech and financial services in order to repay the student loan debt. These factors could disrupt the U.S. economy in the next 10 years.

Chapter 10: Pay Off Your Highest Balance

First

Paying off your lowest balance on your credit card first feels like the most practical option to boost your credit score. Yes, that's true, but only if you are looking at a long-term strategy. However, if you want to boost your credit score within a month, you need to take the hard target first. That's right, paying off your highest balance first should be your first priority to boost your credit score within 30 days. If you carry a monthly balance on one of your credit card accounts, chances are that you do the same on all your other credit cards. Different cards would have different interest rates and the one with your highest balance will be eating away all your money and pulling down your credit score.

On the other hand, if you start focusing on paying off your largest balance first, it would give you greater merit because you are slicing away one of the biggest debts in your credit history and it directly affects your credit score. Of course, this can be tough to achieve, but proper planning and management skills is the right way to get this done.

With this strategy you start increasing the payment of the credit card with the largest balance and the highest APR, while still continue to make minimum payments on the rest of your credit cards. Within time, you will notice that you have paid off your balance on the card with the highest APR, and then it becomes easier for you to move on to the card with the second highest balance and so on.

A good way to get started is to pay double or even triple your minimum payment on the card with the highest balance.

Consolidating Your Debts

If you want to make your things simple, the best way is to consolidate your debt into a single loan or card. This means that you have to make a single payment every month rather than four or five. You can also automate your payments so that you do not have to worry about any late payments.

The biggest advantage of consolidating your debt is that you do not have to worry about four or five different interest rates. You would be paying only one APR for your entire balance, which may be lower to the total accumulated APRs of all your credit cards.

Chapter 11: Improving Your Credit Score

There are several approaches you can take to improving your credit. For the best results and the greatest likelihood of seeing positive change fast, employ as many of them as possible.

Tip 1: Use Section 609 of the FCRA to File a Dispute

As I talk about in my book **The Section 609 Credit Repair Solution**, Section 609 of the Fair Credit Reporting Act (FCRA) puts the burden of providing proper documentation on the credit bureaus.

By filing a dispute letter with the FCRA that highlights key technicalities (for example, the lender not sending the credit application to the three credit bureaus, or your identify not being verified before the information is included), you can have negative items removed quickly.

For all the details on how to employ this strategy including four dispute letter templates, **download The Section 609 Credit Repair Solution**.

Tip 2: Dispute any existing errors

If there are any errors or inaccuracies in your credit report, you don't always have to go to the lengths of writing a letter and quoting Section 609. You can talk to the parties involved and try to get it figured out. For example, if you have an outstanding medical bill from an urgent care facility that you were under the impression your insurance company would cover, contact your insurance company to have it addressed. The unpaid bill is likely affecting your credit score.

Repairing your reports is the central element in re-establishing good credit. Seven out of 10 people report having at least one inaccurate or negative credit item that need to be removed or corrected.

Tip 3: Pay Down Your Debt

After having negative items removed, the next step to a good credit score is to pay down the debt that you have. Lenders are interested in not only how well you pay on your accounts but also in the total amount of debt that you have. This is responsible for 30% of your score.

If you have multiple sources of debt and are looking to reduce interest fees, start by paying down the debt with the highest interest rate.

Tip 4: Don't Wait to Pay

The single largest component of a credit score is your payment history. If you are late on or skip payments on items such as credit cards or vehicle loans, your score will surely be affected. This is true for instalment debt payments (such as television) and any of your monthly bills, such as your utilities. This is because of many merchants, not just lenders, report payment patterns to credit bureaus.

You don't have to wait for your credit card bill to come around once a month in order to pay your bills. You always have the option to pay earlier in the month, or even several times a month, if you have larger purchases and want to keep your balance down.

Tip 5: Lower your Interest Rate

If you are looking for ways to improve your credit score, having a lower interest rate on your credit card can help. Creditors believe that accounts with lower interest rates are associated with better-qualified individuals and will look at you as being a better risk for them to deal with.

Talking your creditors into giving you a lower rate can be done with a four-step process that is simple and easy to follow. Here's how:

Find out what rate you are paying. You may have signed up for the card with an introductory rate that is now much higher. Go online or look at your statement to see your current interest rate.

Google your card company and credit card to see what type of rate is being offered to new customers.

Check your credit score to see what your interest rate should be. Don't accept 29.9% if you deserve a 14.9% rate.

Ask your card company to lower your rate. Armed with all of the above information, simply call the customer service number listed on the back of your card or your statement and present your case why your interest rate should be lowered.

Often, simply by following these steps and calling your credit card company, you will be able to cut your rate in half. This could save you hundreds or thousands of dollars a year, depending on the size of your accounts.

To take this one step further, if you're able to secure a personal loan or line of credit with a low interest rate, or if you already have one, pay off your credit card debts with this account. Then you'll be paying a lower interest rate on these debts.

Tip 6: Focus on Getting Rid of New Debt

Far too many people focus their energy on trying to erase debt from years ago. This can be seen as good debt, as it shows that you paid it off consistently over time if that is the case. Newer debt has more of an impact on your credit score, so make getting rid of that debt your primary focus.

Tip 7: Apply for a Credit Limit Increase

You've probably heard that it's best to stay under 50% of your credit limit on all cards, sometimes even below 30%. If you have some expensive purchases coming up, or you simply require more charges to be put on your credit card, talk to your credit card company about an increased credit card maximum to keep your percentage in check.

Tip 8: Avoid Opening New Credit Cards for One Year

Inquiries from creditors are automatically deleted from your record after twelve months. This technique is especially helpful if your credit report currently shows a high number of inquiries. That fact, in and of itself, may be the major reason for a lower than necessary credit score.

Tip 9: Keep any Search for New Credit to Within a Short Time Period

Focus any search on obtaining new credit within a short period, such as one month. The number of inquiries from lenders in your credit bureau file negatively affects your credit score. If the inquiries all come in within thirty days (for a car loan, for example), they will all be recognized as part of one search. If, however, you spread your search over several months, the pattern will look like multiple searches: a negative in most credit scoring systems.

Tip 10: Limit the Number of Inquiries

Too many inquiries into your credit can hurt your credit, so limit how often you reach out to potential lenders. In other words, limit how many credit products you apply for.

Tip 11: Follow a budget

To achieve ongoing success managing your finances, learning to budget is key. Work out a budget that will enable you to make more than the minimum payment on your cards every month. You may also have to deprive yourself of some purchases and make necessary lifestyle adjustments. You should try as much as possible to buy only items that are necessary. Discretionary purchases should be left out until you have extra money to spend.

In Closing

Do check your credit score periodically, perhaps every six months or so while you are working to rebuild your credit score. Your inquiries do not negatively impact your credit score. Make sure you get your score directly from the credit bureaus or FICO to ensure they aren't counted as lender inquiries.

Maintaining a good credit score is extremely important, so don't discount the ability of any one of these methods to have an impact on your credit score. Credit scores are more of a big picture, so small steps toward a better credit score really do add up. Follow these tips to ensure that all debt and bad credit decisions are in the past, and that a solid credit score is in your future.

Chapter 12: Understanding Credit

Generally, the credit score number everyone is concerned with is the FICO credit score, which ranges from 300 to 850. The higher your score, the more likely lenders will want you to borrow money from them, and the better interest rates they'll offer. For example, a mortgage of $165,000 amortized over 30 years with a 3.98% interest rate will have a monthly principle and interest payment of $785 and you will pay $117,900 in interest over the life of the loan. Contrarily, the same mortgage amount with just 60 basis points more in interest or 4.58% will have a monthly principle and interest payment of $785 and you will pay $138,801 in interest over the life of the loan. This same example when applied to a mortgage of $265,000 at 3.98% interest will have a monthly principle and interest amount of $1,190 compared to $1,278 at 4.58% and you will pay $178,637 in interest over the life of the loan at the lower rate compared to $210,304 in interest. Those difference in interest rates could be the difference in 30-40 points in credit ratings. Similarly, you may want to consider the somewhat less tradition 15 year mortgage, where possible to eliminate some of that large interest paid number.

What makes up a credit score

Rebuilding bad credit isn't easy. It takes time, for one thing. Payment history is the factor weighted most heavily in calculating your scores. On-time payment history accounts for roughly 35% of your credit score, and late payments are reported on credit reports for seven years. Over time, negative information carries less weight (provided current bills are paid on time). In the credit world, you are not late until you are 30 days late. A creditor may apply a late fee to your account, but will not report you late to a credit bureau until you are more than 30 days late. Paying your bills on time is the only way to guarantee your high score, but there are other major factors that come into play in the credit score algorithm. For example, the amount of debt you have counts for about 30% of your score. It is for this reason, you may have heard someone say you should make at least one extra payment on your car or house note a year. That extra payment should be applied directly to the principle amount you owe, thus reducing the amount of debt you have.

Let's take this a step further and look at a way you can manipulate your credit card debt in a way that will deliver points to your score. Let's say in January at the end of your credit billing cycle, you have an outstanding balance of $700. You pay some amount on the bill, use the card during the month of February, and at the end of the February billing cycle, your balance is $600. The formula for calculating your score will recognize a $100 decrease in the amount of debt you have. Let's say in March, at the end of your billing cycle your outstanding balance is $500 and $400 in April. Each month the formula will give you points for paying down the amount of debt you owe. In order to add these points to your score, you have to know when your billing cycle ends for each of your credit cards. Then pay down your balance before the billing cycle ends so that each month your outstanding balance is reported lower and lower. From my experience, credit card companies report your balance on the same day each month. So once you know the day your balance will be reported, you can manipulate your score and your outstanding balance by paying down the amount of credit card debt reported. In the end, this will help you realize a few extra points on your score month over month.

Another element of your credit score is the length of time you have used credit. This accounts for about 15% of your score, and helps lenders better understand your ability to maintain credit accounts over a period of time. If you are new to using credit do not fret your short credit history.

Paying your bills on-time constantly and consistently will outweigh having a long credit history with inconsistent payment history. Pay your bills on time. In addition to having positive credit over a period of time, the type of credit ,and where you get your money from matters as well. For example, borrowing money from a pay day lender will not have the same positive impact as opening a new account with a more reputable lender such as a traditional bank or credit union. This is because the formula recognizes you are borrowing from one source and not the other primarily based on your inability to qualify for more traditional underwriting standards of banks or credit unions. This goes back to the lower interest rates you can demand with a higher credit score. Typically pay day lenders are lending money with much higher interest rate than you can get from a traditional financial institution. Nowhere in your credit score does it reward you for paying interest on your balance. While maintaining a consistent payment history will help your score in the long run, doing business with subprime lenders such as pay day lenders does not have the same .positive impact as opening a new account at a bank such as Wells Fargo. New credit lines do indeed account for a small amount of your credit score, roughly 10%, so be aware of this when you begin establishing new credit lines. If you are unable to meet traditional banking underwriting guidelines for approval, you may want to consider opening a secured account, and we will discuss this strategy in detail later.

Three credit reporting agencies

There are three main credit bureaus, and they are TransUnion, Experian, and Equifax. It is wise to know each of your scores, because they may be a different number at each bureau. This is because not all creditors report to all three credit bureaus. So you may have an outstanding loan with a local bank reporting your account to Experian and TransUnion, but not Equifax. In this scenario, let's suppose you have this account for 10 years with no late payment history. Your Equifax score will not reflect this positive account, and may be lower than TransUnion and/or Experian.

If you chose to monitor your score using myfico.com you will also realize there are multiple types of credit scores depending on the type of purchase you are making will depend on which score is used. There is a score creditors request when you are requesting a credit card account and there is a different score used when you are want to borrow money to purchase a home. So, if you are increasing your credit to become eligible for a mortgage loan, you will want to make sure you are not monitoring your auto loan score. While establishing or re-establishing a good credit record, it is important that you monitor your scores. This does several things for you. One, it allows you to see what activities are having the most impact on your score. For example, when you are monitoring your credit score with a website such as myfico.com, you will receive an update each time your score changes. You will then know why the score changed based on new information reported by each bureau. So then, when positive things happen, you will know to increase that activity, and when negative things happen, you will know to watch out for that.

Chapter 13: What To Do About Negative Reports

Now that you know what your creditors are saying about you, it's time to start working on changing that image. You've already marked your report with the blatant mistakes that are bringing your score down and now is the time to do something about them.

Errors in Personal Information

You might not think that something as simple as a wrong address is a problem, but it can be one of the biggest threats to your credit score there is. It could be an indication that someone is using your credit and having things sent to a totally different address. It could also put you on notice that the creditor or the credit bureau has mixed up your file with someone else's, perhaps someone with a similar name to yours.

Any mistakes on your report, no matter how minor they seem, need to be addressed. Those inaccuracies can present a problem later on. For example, when you make a request for your report, the credit bureau will ask you to verify your identity. They will ask you questions based on what's in your report, so if the information you give does not match with what they have on file, you may be blocked from gaining access to it in the future.

So, what can you do about these errors when you catch them? That depends on where in the report you find it. If the mistake is in the header, you need to file a dispute with the credit bureau. How you file the dispute will depend on which credit bureau report you have.

There are three major credit bureaus, Equifax, Experian, and TransUnion. Each one will have a different system for disputing errors. The best way to find out how to handle them is by visiting their website, or you can visit The Consumer Financial Protection Bureau for instructions on how to submit your dispute.

Credit card accounts and loans: When analyzing the details of credit card accounts and loans, make sure that you check the creditor name on the account. Sometimes the names can be different from the actual creditor you have your account with. This can happen if the business you have established credit with is owned by another company or if it has a parent company it is associated with. Still, you want to make sure that the name is of a legitimate creditor, which might mean you'll have to contact them to determine what is the actual case.

Sometimes you can verify what company it is by the date the account was opened or other clues. At any rate, you want to be absolutely sure that the creditors listed are those that you have legitimate accounts with.

Duplicate Accounts: Occasionally, some accounts may be listed on your report twice. This is something you will have to correct as soon as possible. Duplicate accounts can make you appear to be overextended in debt. There are times, however, when duplicate accounts are actually legitimate as in the case of refinancing a loan or when you re-open a card after it has been stolen. Before you contact the company, make sure you have checked all possible options beforehand.

If you discover that there is no legitimate reason for the duplication, you should file a dispute with the credit bureau requesting the debt to be investigated.

Errors in the Collection of Public Records Section of the Report: It goes without saying, anything in the collection section of your report can have a major impact on your credit score. These are accounts that are so far past due that they've found their way to a debt collector, which will automatically have serious repercussions.

These accounts are often difficult to understand because they may end up being bought and sold by several different collection agencies. You may have no idea which agency has your debt at any particular time, but it is important for you to do some detective work and find out. Mistakes often happen when accounts are transferred from one agency to another. Enough discrepancies associated with one account may be enough to convince the credit bureau to delete the whole thing altogether.

Any type of overdue bill can appear in this section. They could range from medical bills for services you thought were covered by insurance, subscriptions you thought were canceled or bills you just forgot about. This is a common occurrence for those who may have moved a lot over the years.

If you don't know what the bill is for, contact the debt collector and find out who the original creditor was. Ask for a phone number if one is not listed on the report. Call the creditor and request them to send you a "validation notice." This is a written proof that the debt is yours.

If the error is in your public records, verify that the judgment is correct. If you have paid any amount on the judgment, then it should be reflected in the report, or if the amount of the judgment is not correct, then you must file a dispute.

Inquiries: Pay extra special attention to inquiries because if they are not legitimate applications for credit applied for by you, they would be a clear indication that someone is trying to get credit in your name. If there are any inquiries on your report that you didn't ask for, notify the credit bureau immediately and request a freeze. This will automatically go into effect and stop any identity thieves from opening new accounts in your name.

You should also notify the creditor to let them know that you did not apply for credit and that someone is trying to use your identity to get credit. If done quickly enough, it should stop the thief from any more attempts to use your credit.

What Are Your Options

When you find errors on your report, you have several options. One of the first things you want to do is to file a dispute with the credit bureau. Since the information contained in their reports is used to measure your credit score, you want to notify them first so that they can take whatever steps are necessary to verify the information and correct it. Once corrected, this will automatically boost your score.

Your next option is to address the issue with the creditor directly. When you make the dispute in writing, the creditor is required by law to investigate it and make corrections. They must not only notify you and the credit bureau where an error is found, but they must also notify the other credit bureaus of the error so that your report can be corrected.

What to do About Legitimate Negative Marks

After you have dealt with the mistakes on your credit report, your next step is to address the legitimate negative marks. One of the first things you should do is start to pay off these debts as soon as possible. This may mean entering into negotiations with the creditors to remove the items listed in your report.

You could simply just offer to pay the delinquent amount and be done with it, but since this type of item can stay on your report for years, paying it off will not improve your score very much. In that case, there are several different things you can do.

Pay for Delete: A pay for delete request is an offer to pay off the debt in full, in return, the creditor agrees to remove the negative mark from your credit report. This is a win-win situation where the creditor gets his money, and you get to clear their negative mark. While all creditors will not accept this type of offer, it is worth a first try.

A Goodwill Request: If the bill has already been paid, then there is no incentive for the creditor to remove the mark from your report. In that case, you could draft a letter to the creditor, explaining why you fell behind in your payments and how you've corrected your circumstances and respectfully request them to change their report to reflect your change. Again, no creditor is required to do this, but it is an option that some will be willing to accept.

Wait it Out: When those two options fail, your next best thing is to wait it out. The law only allows for negative information to remain on your report for seven years (ten years in the case of bankruptcy). The advantage of this is that the older information weighs less on your overall credit score than more recent information. So, if you have a negative mark that is six years old, it is not likely to carry much weight on your report than something that is reported in the last six months.

But waiting and doing nothing is not always the best way to go. There are plenty of other things you could do while waiting. Use that time to add some more positive things to your credit report. By making regular payments, on time, you can start pulling your score up, and you'll gradually begin to see improvement.

Don't be Fooled

Many credit repair companies will try to convince you that bankruptcy is an easier way to boost your score, but they would be decidedly wrong. While bankruptcy is probably the fastest way to get out of debt, it won't remove any of the negative marks on your credit report.

What bankruptcy will do for you is to discharge your debt. The balances will all be listed as $0, but the accounts to which you owed money to will remain as a negative mark on your report. And those accounts that were included in the bankruptcy judgment will be reported accordingly.

Others might also convince you that all you have to do is close an account and the negative reports will just disappear. This can also be misleading. Anytime you close an account with a balance remaining, the creditor will still report your bill is delinquent until you bring it current or you pay it off in full. Closing an account does absolutely nothing to boost your credit score; it will only prevent you from using it.

Even paying off a past due balance will not remove any negative marks on your report. When you pay the balance due, it will change the status from 'past due' to 'current.' As long as there is no charge-off or collection related to the account, it will not be recorded as delinquent. However, if there is a charge off or a collection, it will remain on your report even if you completely clear the debt.

Whether the information on your credit report is a result of error or it's a legitimate mark on your credit history, some things can be done to remove it. Regardless of where the negative mark comes from, the good news is that the law is firmly on the side of the consumer. Credit bureaus are required to provide accurate information and must have a dispute process in place so you can repair any damage to your credit score without hassle.

If you find the need to dispute an item and the credit bureau is unable to verify its accuracy, the item must be removed from your report within 30 days after the dispute has been received. This means that no matter what is in your report today, the worse case scenario is that it will disappear within just a few years.

Writing the Dispute Letter

Writing a dispute letter can be difficult and unnerving. You're worried that you're going to get a negative response, or you just won't be able to word it professionally to warrant the attention you seek. However, you do have options when it comes to getting that letter done.

Some people, not trusting their own writing abilities, may opt to hire a credit repair company to write the letter for them. For this, however, they will charge a fee, and if you're already dealing with credit problems, it could put you back even more financially.

If you do choose to use a credit repair company, be careful about which one you choose. Many of them are frauds and will offer you more than they can possibly deliver. You should expect the company representative to be very specific in outlining exactly what they can and cannot do for you.

It is beneficial to know that no credit repair company can promise you a specified increase in points on your credit report. If any do so, run in the opposite direction as fast as you can. This is illegal and will bring you more trouble in the end. They can never ask for payment up front for their services, so you should be wary of any service that does this. You should only be expected to make payment after their services have been provided.

Credit repair companies are not always necessary to write your dispute letter. In fact, there is nothing they can offer you that you can't do yourself. However, if you have a credit report with a lot of errors or you're dealing with issues related to identity theft, you might be able to benefit from their expertise. Those who choose them generally are those who just don't have a lot of time to go through the dispute process on their own. They recognize that credit repair companies can get the letters written, and other issues addressed much more quickly and for them, it is worth paying the extra fee.

If you decide to write the letter yourself, some simple guidelines can help you to write an effective dispute letter.

Get to the point. Your letter should be clear and concise, identifying exactly what you found wrong. Include the date of the error, the account, and the lender.

Don't refer to the law. They already know the laws relating to dispute so just pointing out the error should be sufficient.

Include a reliable return address so they can respond to you in a timely manner.

Your dispute letter does not have to be a long explanation of what you think is wrong. As long as you stipulate exactly where the error lies and why you feel that way it should be adequate enough to warrant at least an investigation.

It should be worded and addressed like any other business letter and sent to the correct address listed on the credit bureau's account. Follow the guidelines listed on their website, and your letter should get the proper attention it deserves.

Chapter 14: Credit Repair Agencies

Now, if you have already been thinking about repairing your credit history for quite some time, chances are you have been looking for "professional" help in the form of credit repair agencies. You see advertisements in newspapers, the Internet and on television. You probably have been spammed by their offers if you left your contact details with one of them. You probably have been promised things like: "New credit identity – 100% Legal!" or "Sparkling clean credit history in 30 days!".

Do yourself a favor and handle it yourself. While some of the credit agencies might be sincere in helping the average person out, they are only a handful. When things seem too good to be true, they probably are! The truth is – only prudent debt repayment plan and consistent credit repairing effort can improve your credit history.

What is Card Segregation?

If someone offers you a credit repair plan that will segregate your credit history by applying for an Employer Identification Number, beware! They will tell you an EIN can be used instead of your SSN to establish a new credit history. However, if you default your bills and your creditors discovers that you hold a bad credit record under the other SSN account, you may be charged for felony fraud and be liable for a lawsuit. So, don't play with fire!

Of course, the most sensible course of action is to dispute all the listings on your own and do not try to pull of any tricks that seems illegal.

In fact, you need to understand that you can do every service that a credit repair firm can do for free or at a very low cost. Nobody is able to legally remove true and accurate information from your credit report. Lastly, there is no miracle cure for bad credit! Do not spend the unnecessary money on credit repair agency when cash flow is what you need most at this point in time.

Protecting Your Credit

Hopefully after some time, you are able clear some of the blemishes that are on your credit report. It's completely fine if you find it tough to remove everything. Over time, all records will be erased and you will always have a chance to start fresh. To be able to maintain this clean slate, there are many things which you need to do.

1) Protect Your Credit

Credit is one of the most important assets you possess. The difference between having credit or no credit can be the difference between the freedom of choice and the feeling of suffocation. With that said, you definitely should protect your credit.

- When traveling, don't leave the car rental agreement inside the car where car thieves can easily access.

- When shopping, do not write your address and phone number on credit receipts. Never allow any cashier or clerk to write down your credit card number or personal details on a piece of paper.

- When surfing the web, make sure that your payment method is secure. (Buy from trusted websites and vendors) You should also delete the browser cookies after shopping online. Many of these websites store sensitive information in cookies so that it makes it easier for you to shop again in the future. However, this opens you up to the vulnerability of phishing attacks, which aim to obtain your cookies in which your details are contained.

2) Review Credit Card Statements

This is a crucial step which needs to done regularly. Reviewing statements allow you to catch unauthorized use of your accounts and be able to notify the credit companies quickly.

3) Review Your Credit Report Once Every 6 Months

It is a best practice to review your credit report once every 6 months to ensure that you are not a victim of identity theft. All consumers should be able to pull out a copy of their credit report once every year for free. If you find that you might have been a victim of identity theft, do not panic. Follow the steps mentioned in the Credit Repair chapter to inform the agencies of this issue and file disputes on the erroneous listings.

4) Clean up Your Mailing List

Junk (physical) mails are extremely annoying. More often than not, you just chuck them into the bin without even opening up the envelope. However, doing this run the real risk of having someone steal your discarded mail and applying for credit cards on your behalf. This is essentially identity hijacking. You can protect yourself by removing your name from the credit agencies mailing list. To do so, simply dial in to the agency hotline or write to them via physical mail.

Chapter 15: How To Repair Your Bad Credit Quickly But Effective – Additional Methods To Help You Get Your Credit Moving

If you have been finding that you are simply struggling to improve your bad credit and feel as though you are at a dead end, don't despair yet! There are actually many quick but effective ways of tackling problem credit.

Just because your credit score doesn't look very promising, that doesn't mean to say there is nothing you can do to stop it from improving it and making it healthier. Here are some simple but effective tips to help get you started.

Pay Off Bad Debts

There might be one or two debts that stretch back a good few years that still need to be paid off. If there is, you need to get rid of these as quickly as possible.

You do not want bad debts piling up against you and being left unpaid because it will just damage your credit. So, the first thing you want to do is call up your creditors and find out how much you owe still.

It might be possible to get some of the debt reduced but don't get your hopes up, very few companies will do this. Every company is different in how they work and they might find that if it is a smaller debt, they could cancel it or make lower payment options. If you can get however, the debt reduced and paid off, it will help to boost your credit, even if it's just a little, every little helps.

Take A GOOD Look at Your Credit Reports

You've already heard this before but it is important. You do need to keep reviewing and re-reading your credit reports so that if there are any errors you can pick them up. To be honest, you can easily miss a few errors the first time around but that is why you should review the reports a good few times just so if there are any errors, you can find them.

Of course, this can actually help you to improve your bad credit because if there are errors, you can ask for them to be removed. That can in fact help to improve your credit in many ways and of course; having a good and error free report is always useful in the long run.

Choose To Set Payment Reminders

You probably are busy running a household and at times it can be very easy to forget one or two bills need to be paid. However, missing payments on your bill is the best way to hurt your credit. You don't want to miss any payments, so pay on time because it all counts to your payment history!

Remember, at least thirty five percent of your credit score is made up because of your payment history. If you have a good payment history then your credit can be in a good shape soon enough, if not, it will never improve.

If you are struggling to remember to pay, set out a payment reminder or better still, give permission for the bank to automatically send the payment each month out of your account. This is much better because you can be assured the payment goes out without being a day or two late.

Avoid Credit Cards

A lot of people do end up with seven or eight credit cards which mean the ability to rack up even more debt. A great way to keep the credit score good and improve upon it is to avoid using credit cards. I know this is going to be difficult for many of you to do but actually, it's very important to help improve on your bad credit!

Of course, you might not take too much notice of not using credit cards. So, if you are using credit cards, try to limit the amount you charge and try to limit the amount of cards you have also. Don't have five or ten, try to keep to only two or three at the most! The more cards you have, the more debt you can have so just stick to a few.

Keep temptation down to a minimum.

Build Good History with a Secured Credit Card

If you are looking for a quick way to really boost your credit, why not use a secured credit card? This can actually be a fantastic way to improve your scores because you do not charge more than what you can afford.

So, for example, you can place a certain amount with the credit card and the bank, say two hundred dollars, you use the card like a normal credit card but once you have spent that two hundred, the card is done. You don't pay at the end of the month because you have paid as you've gone along.

This is a great way to really boost your credit and it helps you to avoid spending money you simply do not have. You can reuse the card by adding more money into your account and it can be a good way to boost credit. Though, interest can vary with these cards so be wary before you choose these.

Call the Creditors

If you can do this as soon as you realize you have debts you simply cannot afford to pay back, it can be very good. Calling your creditors can be great because they will help to find a good resolution in ensuring both sides are happy. They might even be happy to know they are getting ten dollars a week, remember, just as long as the debt is being paid back, most creditors will be happy.

Again, I've mentioned this above before but it's important because the quicker you do this, the less it will impact on your credit. It will still have a bearing on your credit but not as much. What is more, you can at times, come to an agreement with your creditors about the payment schedules. So let's just say your credit card company is asking for fifty or sixty each month but you simply cannot afford that each month, you could ask to lower the payments to twenty.

You can explain the situation, saying you cannot afford to pay a high repayment schedule each month. Most creditors are willing to negotiate as long as they can still get their money, so most of the time, they will lower the payment so that you can afford to repay.

Use the Snowball Method

To get rid of your debt faster and really improve your credit score, why not try the old snowball method? This is where you decide to pay off one debt at a time, you would usually start with the smallest amount of debt – that way you can pay off the debt faster – and continue to pay off each debt one at a time.

It's the snowball method which allows you to keep on rolling as soon as you start with debt repayments. Though, you could start with the most costly debt first if you would like and tackle that but of course, it's your choice!

Fast Fixes

Use An Installment Loan As Your Next Loan...

Now, instantly you think this isn't right, not when you are trying to get out of debt. However, if you really have to take up a loan or you wish to purchase a new car or take out a mortgage, an installment loan is the way to go.

These types of loans can actually be really great. The reason why is because you can build a period of stable payment history which is of course going to help improve your scores. So, let's just say that you wanted to purchase a new car and you were to take an installment loan, you could build your credit by offering a good form of payment history.

If You Have To Use Cards Use Them Wisely and Pay Them Off Quickly

Just say you have a few credit cards and have a balance on them, you will want to get that balance back down to zero as fast as you can. It can be very good for your credit and overall, it's wise to keep them down to the bare minimum.

Having a zero balance can look good but the likelihood you will use them again is looming so when you do use them, try to keep the balance as low as possible. Keeps the balance low and at the end of the month, try to pay it off then also that way should you need to use them again the next month, you don't have a big bill to pay.

Know Your Limitations

Keeping your credit at a good level and keeping it healthy can only be achieved when you know your limitations. If you don't, you could end up spending money you don't have and can't afford to pay back which ultimately hurts your credit. So, if you have to spend extra money, spend wisely and don't go overboard.

If you have an emergency then fair enough but don't use your cards unless it's for an emergency – a real one. Don't use your cards to purchase any knick knacks for you, only emergencies.

Use an Old Card

If you have an old charge card or credit card somewhere that you don't often use, you could dig that out if you really have to use them. You have a long payment history with these which could be good for your overall credit history. Though, that doesn't mean you should charge thousands.

If you have to charge things on these, keep them low amounts and pay back immediately at the end of the month. Remember, companies will continue to update these cards on your credit report which can be good for you.

Ask For Redemption

Some creditors can be very nice indeed. If you have been a loyal customer to a store or somewhere in which you owe money to, you could get some goodwill from them. Now, just say you have made one or two late repayments, if you have been a good customers to the lender, you could ask if they could erase the late payment – if you do achieve this, your credit score can be really good.

This might take a little longer than what you hope; every lender is different so you might find it takes weeks or even months.

However, it can be good for your overall credit if one or two late payments are erased.

Avoid Several Loans At Once

A really important point to remember is that you don't want several loans appearing on your credit history all at once. This looks bad because in the eyes of many, it seems as though you cannot handle your finances. Lenders don't like to see people with hundreds of loan applications at the same time, so try to find one loan that handles all of your needs.

Vote!

This might sound a little strange but being on the electoral roll that actually helps to boost your credit score. You can register to vote but if you don't want to vote, you don't need to but being on the electoral roll can be good for your credit.

Build Your History

Future lenders do want to see how well you have been able to handle your money. Even if your credit isn't filled with many loans that doesn't automatically mean it's great either. Having little or no credit history can be really bad at times because your credit score can be low simply because there is nothing there to tell people much about your lending history.

Avoid Credit Improving Companies

At times, you can see a lot of companies out there that promise to help you to boost your credit history. However, this isn't always the best solution for you. You can at times find that the companies take your money but don't do much for your credit – not all are like this but it might be better to avoid.

You could try them if you really wanted to of course. However, why not try boosting your credit by yourself? There are many methods for you to do this and to be honest; if you take some advice from the above methods you could find that dealing with your credit is simple.

Simple Tips to Help Keep Your Credit at a Good Level

· Budgeting Your Household Finances And Cash

· The Amount Of Money You Borrow

· Saving Money For The Future

· Insuring Your Life In Every Which Way Possible

So, first of all, let's start with budgeting. This is something most homes should be doing because it can be very difficult to get anywhere without setting out some proper budget rules. If you don't even know what money is coming in or out of your home, you are in deep trouble.

You absolutely need to take note of everything that is coming in to your home and the money that goes out of it as well. There can be lots of bills so you don't always know the right amount, so take time to figure out these things and set out a monthly budget for your home as well.

When it comes to borrowing money, try to keep the loan to the lowest amount possible. You might think you should take a few extra thousand dollars just in case of emergencies or to put away for a rainy day but in the long run, it's not great. The more you borrow, the more you pay and if you borrow extra money you don't necessarily need, it's a waste.

Instead, borrow small amounts so that you can be assured you will be able to repay the loans back. If you take out huge amounts at one time, you can often find yourself struggling to repay.

When it comes to saving for the future, it can be really good and wise in fact. You can always put away a few extra cents every now and again or when you have extra cash. Doing this will help you to avoid taking out more money than you need to later on.

Of course, you might not think you would be able to save up for a rainy day but actually putting a little money away every so often can prove to be great. You never know when you need cash and saving for the future is important no matter how small it may seem.

A last point to remember is that even if you have poor credit, you should still take out insurance. Many of you do forget and something happens which knocks you off balance. What is more, if you aren't fully insured for your health the debt can go on your credit report; same with auto accidents. If you have a car accident and aren't fully insured, you could be left with a lot of debt.

That is why it is going to be so important to know each and every method possible to help you boost and improve your bad credit. It is possible and even though it may seem to be a challenge, it can be possible to change.

Chapter 16: Should You Use A Credit Repair Company?

While there can be a fair amount of work involved in undertaking to repair your credit yourself, it can certainly save you a great deal of money AND help you see the wider picture when it comes to your personal finances. It can also get you into the habit of taking your money seriously and devoting time to money management to build a more solid and secure financial future for you and your family. Just think, once you resolve any credit issues you may have, you can use the time and the money you will save to start learning more about investments and beginning to build real assets that will really put your money to work earning more for you. This in turn will help you achieve the long term goals you have set for yourself, such as a college fund for each child and retirement at an early enough age to enjoy it and be financially

comfortable   too.
There is no shortage of companies willing to take on your credit repair chores for you. They are one of the few businesses that are booming in a down economy, along with resume services offering help to all those desperate for a job. There are also plenty of companies that do a bad job and the bare minimum, with a few who are   notably   conscientious. This is one of those times that it pays to be very thorough in your research. If you do decide that the only way to tackle the mountain of debt you are dealing with is to use one of these services, compare not just costs, but look for real reviews from real people. Get testimonials, learn about others' experiences and then decide if the cost   is   justified. The other issue to keep in mind is that there are limitations with credit repair firms. Firstly, depending on which state you are in, you might or might not be allowed to use these services. Secondly, some of these services are only able to operate   in   certain   states.

They also might not offer a full service. Some will only dispute a few items per month, so if you have a credit report full of errors, the process can take longer to dispute every negative item that you wish to have removed.

Typically, you will be charged a monthly fee in return for a specified amount of work. Obviously, the longer they drag out the process, the more money they will earn, money which might be better used to pay down your debts.

You can speed up your own process by using the templated form letter and tracking sheets we have discussed, and by following up promptly. You can have replies within 35 days in most cases, one way or the other, and then follow up as needed to get the results you want. While the best credit repair companies do a good job, they can't do any better than you can do yourself, and you will still have to spend time following up with them if they ask for more information and so on. No one will ever take more of an interest in your financial affairs than you will, so unless you are really too busy or overwhelmed, roll up your sleeves and do the work yourself.

If you are in partnership, another approach might be to delegate the chore to one spouse and then check in from time to time. Some people were good at mathematics at school and enjoy working with numbers, or are very detail oriented. The spouse with the best abilities in these areas might be the best person to tackle these tasks, but make sure you are BOTH on the same page by checking in regularly on how things are progressing.

One of the reasons people like to use credit repair companies is because they think they have experience and clout with the bureaus when it comes to major issues. This might be true of some of the top ones, but the smaller companies that have sprung up are probably hardly more experienced that you are; they are just seeing an opportunity and taking it. The idea of suing the credit bureaus can be very scary for some people, and not something they want to threaten or then try to take on themselves. While it may sound drastic, it actually happens all the time. If the credit bureau is in violation of the law, it can be fined up to $1,000 per violation. They are rarely willing to go to court and will almost always settle just prior to going before a judge. If they do not settle first, the main thing you must do is show up in court at the appointed time you will be given. Even if you have no lawyer, be sure to make an appearance and do not be intimidated. The credit bureaus will always be present just to see if you show up. If you do not attend, the matter will be dropped. If you do attend and have an impressive-looking file of all your facts with you, they will settle in about 99 percent of cases, and agree to remove all the negative information. You might even be able to get part of the fines from them if you can show that you have a strong case. However, most of the time, the case will never go that far. They will settle and your credit report will be repaired. It may not sound like fun playing "chicken" with credit bureaus in court, but it does work almost all of the time and again, your financial future is to important to not try to repair your credit report and boost your credit score now, so you can start enjoying lower interest rates, more credit availability, and so on. We can't stress this enough. It may be invisible to you most of the time, but your credit score affects ALL areas of your life. Therefore, it is worth it to pursue this matter even if it takes you out of your comfort zone. Again, knowing your rights is the best way to protect yourself and not allow a bad credit report or score or an incorrect credit report to ruin your life for years.

One final area that might affect your credit report is if you have ever used a debt consolidation company. Let's look at this topic in the next section.

Debt Settlement Issues

If you have ever been or still are in way over your head with debts that you do not think you will be able to pay off even after implementing all of the suggestions that we have made at the start of this guide, it is possible to have your unsecured debt, such as credit card, reduced dramatically with the help of debt consolidation companies.

The trouble with some of these companies is that they have not always turned out to be reliable, and in some cases, their failure to pay on time has meant that a credit report has gone from bad to worse even though a person has been attempting to pay down their debts.

This usually happens for two reasons. One might be mismanagement of the account. The second reason is more common, however. It is that the money you pay to them each month and the billing due date on the credit card do not coincide. You pay one lump sum to the debt consolidation company. They then distribute it as needed, according to the terms they have negotiated for you in their deals with each of your creditors. But if one of the dates is earlier than the date you pay them before they start administering the distribution process, you might end up with late fees. The problem with debt settlement is also that often these companies will not take you on as a client unless you are already in trouble, such as 60 or 90 days overdue, in which case, you have already inflicted a great deal of damage on your credit report which it will be difficult to reverse. If you are way behind on your payments, you are likely already hearing from one or more collection agencies, so this will be no surprise to you. In some cases, however, the company can ask that your account be shown as current, removing it from the record as part of the settlement terms and thus improving your credit score and credit report. There is certainly no harm in asking.

Paying down the debts in a systematic way will also prove that you are reliable going forward. Therefore, even if they are not able to remove the damaging information at first, ask if the issue can be revisited in three or six months when you have shown yourself to be capable of sticking to the repayment plan you have been given.

If the debt consolidation company payments are out of synchronization with the card company dates, ask that the date be changed and for a refund of any late fees. Also ask that the account be brought current. Again, point out to them any reason beyond your control as to why you might have fallen into debt, and ask that you not be made to suffer even more with a bad credit score and credit report on top of the problems you might be experiencing.

This also reminds us of one other reason that you might have been late on payments: credit card companies will change their billing cycles and due dates, catching people completely off guard. Billing cycles are rarely calendar months, but anywhere from 28 to 30 days. If they switch from 30 to 28 and you are the type of person who often pays at the last minute, you would get charged with a late fee; therefore, watch your calendar and keep an eye on all statements that will arrive or appear online for any credit card which is in your debt consolidation program. Challenge in writing anything that is unclear.

Some companies are now offering you a choice of dates, but be careful! If you set it to a new date you will end up needing to pay again on that date, which might be only a few days away.

If you do decide to use a debt settlement agency for one or more credit cards or other forms of debt, also be sure to get a written statement for the settlement figure from each creditor so that it does not change over time. An agreement over the phone means nothing. As you would with the credit bureaus, take notes of all discussions with the credit card companies or the consolidation companies as needed and keep them in a safe place for future reference.

The debt consolidation company can help negotiate for you to pay less than the full amount, sometimes as little as 25 percent of what is owed. If you try to negotiate yourself, you will definitely get a good deal if you ask, since what most people do not realize is that debt collectors are always authorized to accept less than the full amount as "payment in full" because getting some money towards the debt is better than getting nothing.

The debt consolidation companies can help, but in most cases they are getting a better deal because you are already obviously having trouble with your payments and again, getting some money is better than nothing from the credit card company's point of view. Look at the fees per month of the debt settlement agency and the duration of the program you will be entering. If you think you can pay down your debt faster by using their monthly fees they would be charging as part of your pay back total each month, then go ahead and start paying down your debt yourself using what you have already learned earlier in this guide.

If you are current with your payments, there is little or no reason for them to settle. Why would they be willing to make a deal if you are already paying on time. The only thing you can consider here is asking for a lower interest rate. If you have been doing your best to pay down your debt and can prove it for your highest interest card, ask them for an interest cut of a few percentage points so that, as you will remind them, you can pay it back even faster. This also works well because your credit to debt ratio will go down more rapidly as well, thus boosting your credit score quickly. This will then put you in a position to ask for a better APR from your other cards as well. Find it intimidating to talk to people like this on the phone? Shoot them an email first to submit this type of request. You can also copy and paste the same request to try to get all of your card APRs lowered. It will only take a few minutes, and even if only one or two say yes, that can still add up to substantial savings. One thing to be very cautious about is any debt settlement figure or mortgage refinance figure. In some cases, you may be responsible for declaring the forgiven amount on your taxes as income. This is only true if the Internal Revenue Service considers you to be solvent, which means that your assets are greater than your debts. People who have tried to walk away from underwater mortgages have found that the amount forgiven has been treated as income, with disastrous results on their tax owed.

Debt consolidation is a strategy that can help you get out of debt, but it can certainly become a negative on your credit report if you do not stay on top of things and make sure you keep good records. It will also not be of great benefit if you do not learn any lessons from your financial difficulties, but start to get into debt once more.

Debt consolidation companies will not usually accept you as a client unless you qualify under their criteria. They will also usually want you to owe a minimum amount, such as $7,500, to qualify. Remember that they will charge a monthly fee for administering your account, which may or may not be worth it if you consider that you could be applying that sum to paying down your debts yourself.

"Ten million dollars after I'd become a star I was deeply in debt."
— Sammy Davis, Jr.

Remember also that even if they are non-profit companies, they are NOT a charity. They still need to make money to pay their employees. Also remember that different companies offer different plans for debt settlement, or so-called debt consolidation. Some will handle credit cards only, while others will deal with mortgage issues, tax liens, medical bills and more. Not all companies will operate in all states so you will want one that is approved in yours. There are no fast fixes for poor credit, no matter what people will tell you. They will usually be in the business of getting you to become a client so they can charge you for the same work you can do yourself if you take the time and get organized. Here is a suggested script you can try to help lower your interest rates, which in turn can help you pay off your debts that much faster:

Once you start paying off your debts regularly on time, you will be taking the final important step in your credit repair process, that of creating new, positive credit. It is not enough to just get rid of the negative information from your credit card, though it certainly helps. The real key is to pay everything on time from now on. This has to be a priority ahead of every other financial consideration in the household, and a priority until you have managed to get your credit score to at least 720.

You will need to be honest about your finances and how you got into trouble in the first place if you were too relaxed about money issues in the past. If it was through no fault of your own, it will help to add new, unblemished credit. Depending on how bad your situation is, your options might be limited, but there are some options still available to you even if your credit score is less than ideal.

Options include:
1-Secured credit cards.
A secured credit card works just like a regular credit card, only you make a deposit with the credit card company. If you deposit $1,000 into your account, then you can have a credit card with a $1,000 limit. These cards aren't ideal, but they can help you repair your credit IF you follow the rules and pay everything off at the end of the month. You get your deposit back when you cancel the card. It will usually have an annual fee as well, so use this option judiciously. You might be better off using that money to pay down all debts.

2-Secured loan.

The bank is happy to loan money if you can provide enough collateral. For instance, if you had $2,000 in your savings account, the bank would be happy to loan you $1,500. However, in this example, you would have to allow them to freeze your savings account until the loan is paid off. On the other hand, if you pay back your loan in a timely manner, then you will be improving your credit. Your loan will naturally come with interest added. Again, this is less than ideal, but better than nothing if you want to start building good new credit.

3-Remember to get a variety of credit. Get a bank loan, a secured credit card, and a store credit card. That would be a simple, but great start. Just be sure to never leave your store card unpaid at the end of the month, since their interest rates can be among the highest in the marketplace generally, let alone for someone who has a poor credit history.

"If you think nobody cares if you're alive, try missing a couple of car payments." – Earl Wilson Whatever methods you decide to use to help create a more positive credit profile, be sure you can pay off your debts at the end of each month. Stick to your budget, review it each month and each quarter, and check your savings accounts to be sure you are on target for the important items on your list. All of this takes time, it is true, but it can be done and you and your family can use the money to start building your financial future on a much more sure footing.

To recap the last couple of chapters, to repair your credit report strategically, you will need to:

1-Minimize the effect of older, negative information.

2-Have negative or incorrect information removed whenever possible.

3-Create new, positive credit.

Choose the solutions that are right for you given your personal circumstances, debts, and amount of time and effort you can spend on this task, versus how much you will have to pay for someone to help you with these matters.

Chapter 17: Get Updates About Credit For Free

I Signed Up For Credit Karma

Credit Karma is a website service that will allow someone to have access to the items that may appear on their credit report just by logging into the Credit Karma website. They also will provide a free credit score. (It's important to note that Credit Karma does not use the FICO Score and has their own method of calculating the credit score they show you.)

You can learn more about the kind of score they use by going to their website and looking at their Frequently Asked Questions. There is a lot of very helpful information on their site.

Credit Karma is a completely free service. They also have a paid service, which I haven't used, if you want to explore this more on their site.

You can find this link and other resources mentioned in this book by going to www.MindfulPressPublishing.com/buy-on-amazon/credit-repair/.

From the Credit Karma About page:

"Credit Karma offers a new way to track your credit score and a unique way to benefit from it. For the first time you can get a truly free credit score with no hidden costs or obligations. Based on your score, you gain access to exclusive offers from companies that value your creditworthiness."

"Our services start with a free credit score. No credit card is required and no strings are attached. Return as often as you like and use our service to track your credit file and stay informed. Credit Karma believes this is a fundamental consumer right. Credit Karma will continue to provide these free credit scores while doing the most to protect your privacy regardless if you use our other services."

In exchange for using their free service, they will provide offers from banks for credit cards that you may qualify for based on your credit score.

This is why I like Credit Karma:

1. They provide a credit score. Even though this isn't the FICO score, it's a credit score that let's me know how I'm doing whenever I log in to the site. If the score is low, something's wrong and needs to be taken care of immediately.

2. There is a section called **My Credit Report Card**. This gives me an A through F grade for Credit Card Utilization, Payment History, Age of Credit History, Total Accounts, Credit Inquiries, and Derogatory Marks. Someone may have a D grade for Age of Credit History while all of the other categories are As and Bs, because they are still waiting for the length of their credit history to "age."

3. Along with the grades that I mention above comes tips for how to improve your credit. For example, my **Total Accounts** grade is a B. When I click on the link to learn more, Credit Karma shows me the

following helpful information which I can use if I want to try to reach an A grade:

"Having a healthy account type mix tells lenders that you are able to handle different kinds of credit and can be beneficial to your credit health. Real estate loans are of the highest credit quality, followed by installment loans, credit cards, and retail cards in order of declining quality. You should aim to keep a mixture of all of these account types on your credit report, with a focus on those of higher quality."

4. There is a section called **Recent Credit Report Activity**. Here I can see what's happening month to month on my credit report such as accounts that have received an increase in spending limit, inquiries made to my credit report, accounts that may have been added to my credit report, etc.

5. There is a section called **My Accounts** where I can see a snapshot of all of my open accounts and their balances.

6. There is a **Credit Score Simulator** that will allow you to enter information about an account you're thinking of opening and the simulator will show you how this new account may affect your credit score.

7. Credit Karma will show recommendations for credit cards or loans that the logged in user may be approved for based on their credit history and rating. My daughter was unable to obtain a credit card due to her lack of credit history, but applied based on a recommendation from Credit Karma and was approved. She's on her way to building a positive credit rating.

There is also a section called **Recent Transactions**, which I am currently not using. I don't need this information at this time so you can decide if it's something you want to access.

When I first joined Credit Karma, I was wondering about security. I found this on their site:

"Credit Karma is committed to your safety. We adhere to industry-leading security precautions to protect your identity and your data. Our privacy policy is verified by TRUSTe. Our security is independently assessed by third parties. We use 128-bit encryption to secure the transmission of personal and financial information to our site, and our servers are physically protected from unauthorized access in a secured location."

Do thorough research to determine if this service is right for you. I find it very helpful, and it may not be for everyone.

Chapter 18: Opting-Out And Overcoming Temptation

In this chapter, you will be discovering all of your Opting-in and Opting-out

options. Surprisingly, you will get your biggest question answered, "Why in

the world am I getting all of these offers in the mail, and how do I get them to stop?"

In this day and time everywhere you turn someone is asking you to sign-up/Opt-in so you can receive this, or sign-up/Opt-in and you will get that. Then there are times you have been signed-up/opted-in without even knowing it.

When thinking of one's options to Opt-in versus Opting-out, as it seems, you will have way more options and opportunities to Opt-in than to Opt-out.

To quickly glance at the advantages of Opting-in one might pose that if you

are in the market for finding a lower costing insurance provider then those offers coming through the mail are right on time. Or, if you were in the market to do a balance transfer from one high interest credit card to another lower interest credit card then the offers have perfect timing.

However, with the advanced technology of the internet, searching for those same offers online will overcome the frustration of shredding countless offers that get shoved into your mailbox.

In turn, the top Opting-out resource to help stop all that continuous begging for your business is – **Optoutprescreen.com.** Optoutprescreen.com is the official consumer credit reporting industry's website to accept and process requests from consumers in order to Opt-in or Opt-out from credit and insurance offers.

The website can help you Opt-out in three ways:

Option #1 – You can Opt-out via phone: 1-(888)-5OP-TOUT
1-(888)-567-8689

Option #2 – You can Opt-out via internet – **www.Optoutprescreen.com**

Option #3 – The third and last option to Opt-out is via mail or written request which is given below.

In addition, there are two types of Opting-out:

Type #1 - Five-year Opt-out Option: This method can be performed via phone 1-(888)-5OP-TOUT or 1-(888)-567-8689 or internet. **[Click Here To Opt-out Five Years]**

Type #2 – To Opt-out permanently: You can process the request online, but you will still have to physically mail out the Permanent Opt-out Election Form. **[Click Here To Opt-out Permanently]**

Moreover, if there is no internet access you can also Opt-out via written request to each of the major Credit Bureaus below:

Experian

Opt Out

P.O.Box 919

Allen, TX 75013

TranUnion

Name Removal Option

P.O.Box 505

Woodlyn, PA 19094

Equifax, Inc.

Options

P.O.Box 740123

Atlanta, GA 30374-0123

Innovis Consumer Assistance

P.O.Box 495

Pittsburgh, PA 15230-0495

The biggest reason you would want to Opt-out is because the more you see offers in your mailbox, the greater the opportunity or temptation you will have if things get financially tough.

The purpose of them sending the credit card offers is not for the good financial times, but for the bad ones. This strategy is similar to Payday Loan Stores. On the flip side, insurance companies use the strategy of annoying you into submission. In spite of both tactics, it is better for you to Opt-out and do the research on your terms, and not theirs!!!

Points to remember:

*Opting-out takes out all the temptation

*All the offers in the mail are waiting for your failure, not thinking about your financial future!

In this last chapter, we will be dealing with the real victims when it comes to debt and the credit crisis. And if you are not a part of the 1% - don't stop reading this book just yet…

Being The Victim Is Very Expensive

In this chapter, you will be exposed to the truth that being poor is very expensive. You will also discover the true definition of wealth and why the present day economy makes it worst for those who are closer to the poverty line, than for those who are not.

The concept of the word "victim" being portrayed in this chapter is referred more on the side of, "One that is not aware of what is really going on."

The Webster Dictionary defines Victim as:

A person who is cheated or fooled by someone else.

As the definition states, the victims are those that were deceived or misled by someone else, usually by someone higher up in position or status. Capitalism is a type of economy, which I believe, the rich capitalize off the poor. In turn, it is in your best interest, not to be the "POOR."

With the unemployment hitting record highs, it exposes the truth that if someone has outstanding debts and the unemployment rates jumps even higher, it will automatically cause a crash. This type of crash implies an economic depression.

Inessence,

whoever is the closest to the poverty line l oses!!!

Just think about, the average car loan is five years, and the average mortgage term is 30 years. If your employment doesn't guarantee **at least** five years, a personal economic crash and depression may be in your future. In this day and time, most companies don't have or rarely promote job security of five years or more. Usually after two years they are trying to replace you with a college graduate waiting to take your position. Not just take your position, but willing to accept half the pay in order to do it.

With this reality so common in many industries, it is very easy to realize that any small hiccup at any time in the economy can cause an enormous negative domino effect. The unique thing about credit is that someone has to be the lender, and someone has to be the borrower.

As I look back over my years of training, I am shocked to admit that only 1% of my training courses have been focused on assisting clients find alternatives to "Untraditional Forms of Borrowing." It is amazing to think that Payday Loan Stores primarily exist in the low-income areas. Conversely, the interest and fees can make it almost impossible not to default which could result in garnishment. The downside of garnishment is that now one has less income to fulfill obligations that they already had, which was not enough to begin with. In essence, not enough income can cause one to make desperate decisions that can mess up one's credit and cash flow.

On the other side, I have also counseled victims that didn't realize that they were victims. I would like to stress this truth.

Investopedia defines Wealth as:

A measure of the value of all the assets of the worth owned by a person, community, company or country. Wealth is found by taking the total market value of all the physical and intangible assets of the entity and then subtracting all debts.

In reality, wealth is not how much money you have, but how much money you have after subtracting all your debts. The sad part of this reality is that probably only 98% of the 99% understand that they fall in the "POOR" category. They believe that since they have access to credit they are well off, when in fact, a single reduction to their available credit would push them back to square one.

Case in point, I have counseled many people who made high incomes while at the same time owing a significant amount of debt. If one loses his /her job and their assets are not more than their liabilities (in this example: student loans), then the person is in trouble. That person is in big trouble because bankruptcy is not an option for the majority of student loans. Now that means you have to pay them back or like a tax lien or child support – they will hunt you down and take it, by all means necessary!!!

I placed this chapter within this book because I wanted to explain to all my readers that the only true way out - is being totally debt free! The POOR is no longer not just having enough, but poverty is not having more than the debts you owe. No matter how much money you have – if your debts outweighs it, you are in danger…

I know that many people have debated me on what I have explained in this last chapter, but for all those that don't agree,

I want to leave you with the definition of victim again: A person cheated or fooled by someone else...

Points to remember:

*Capitalism
is the rich capitalizing off the poor.

*The Poor is no longer not just having enough, but poverty is in fact, not having more than the debts you owe!!!

Chapter 19: Pay On Time

I'd only been a banker a few months when a gentleman walked up to my desk and asked about our home equity line of credit. He was probably in his sixties with a dignified look about him. I imagined he was an accountant or perhaps a doctor and expected his credit would reflect the careful appearance. I was partially right.

When his report came up two things caught my eye. As expected his credit accounts were being handled perfectly: no late payments, low balances, just a few unsecured lines. But his score was easily 100 points lower than both he and I had expected. The culprit was easy enough to find. Though, it was hard to know whether we should laugh about it or cry. His score had taken its drastic fall as a result of a single entry: one $50 collection...from his local library.

You can't ignore anything.

Even a library fine, if not paid on time can turn into bad news.

This is clearly not only about making your debt payments - your credit cards, your auto loans, your mortgage – although it is critical to keep those payments up. Anything that could turn into a collection is potentially reportable to the credit bureaus: medical bills, utilities, online services, even your library fines! It all counts.

The solution appears simple enough:

1.   Bill   comes   in.
2. Pay it.

That's it.

Yet of all the credit related activities we engage in, paying our bills on time is the one activity almost everyone fumbles at one time or another. Many reasons - procrastination, apathy, stress, time-management - play a role in this struggle. But those who successfully pay on time month after month, year after year can all trace their success back to one reason: priorities.

In order to stay on top of your obligations, doing so has to be a priority. It's as simple as that.

Making that happen, however, is hard work. But there are strategies that can be implemented to help.

One strategy is to automate. Thanks to the growing acceptance of online transactions, setting up automatic payments (autopays) with your utilities and online services is commonplace. Autopays are set up when you preauthorize a vendor to pull money from a credit account, or directly from your bank, when your bill is due. Although you may be nervous about providing this type of access, with known entities the risk is minimal. More important is that autopay ensures your payments don't get behind.

But autopay is not without some risks. Because you don't have to write a check each month the amounts you're paying, quietly and out of sight, can be easily forgotten. This can create huge problems if you don't maintain sufficient funds in your bank to cover the amounts that are being pulled. Or, if you spend the money that should be kept in reserve to pay your credit bill, you may find yourself unable to make even the minimum payments when they come due.

Automating your payments does not mean you can then forget about them!

Finally, before setting up any automatic payments be certain that you know exactly how to turn them off. I have heard too many horror stories by clients who have stopped using a service but continue to pay the fees for years, simply because they don't understand the system.

Autopay can be put to great use, but be certain to understand the system and all its pros and cons.

In addition to setting up autopays you can also '**autosave**' for your bills. To do this, simply set up a separate account with your bank which is not used for daily purchases. You can designate a predetermined amount of money to automatically transfer from either your main account, or perhaps directly from your payroll. Your bank should be able to help you put this together. In this way you can be assured that the cash you need to cover your bills, whether paid manually or through autopay, is safely set aside.

Another strategy is to create a 'bill calendar'.

Yes, this is as simple as it sounds. Simply determine what gets paid when and add the entries to whatever calendar you are using. These entries should include both the bills you will pay manually as well as any automatic deductions you have scheduled. If you are using an electronic calendar set your reminders for 24 hours ahead. Then follow through.

It is telling that most of us will schedule a haircut, but few ever schedule a time to manage their financial needs. A bill calendar is an easy step toward real, empowering change.

As I said at the beginning of this chapter, to pay on time is the simplest of all financial activities to get right. But failing to do so is also the most common error. Financial discipline is a hallmark of the wealthy. A simple place to start building that discipline is right here with timely payments.

Recommendations to help you Pay On Time:

1. Make financial timeliness a defining priority. Repeat this to yourself: "I always pay my bills on time!"

2. Set up automatic payments whenever appropriate.

3. Schedule regular times for bill payment and financial management.

4. Don't ignore anything! Remember, even a library fine can turn into bad news.

Chapter 20: Setting Up A Balance Sheet

A balance sheet is used to see where you are financially and what you are worth. The balance sheet is comprised of two sections; 1) the assets and 2) the liabilities.

I set up a separate balance sheet per month and update all of the balances on the same day of each month. This allows me to see whether I am progressing or regressing when it comes to how much I am worth.

1) The Assets – An asset is something that has value. Personally I only count those things that I can sell for cash if needed. Examples are; your car, bank account, collectibles, stocks, the cash value of an insurance policy, etc.

My Assets section may look like this;

Assets	
Checking account	1,800.00
Car value	10,500.00
Savings account	395.00

2) The liabilities – A Liability is a debt that you owe. Examples are; the loan against your car, credit card debt, etc. On my liabilities portion of my balance sheet, I include the following;

1) name of lender

2) last 4 digits of card number

3) interest rate

4) date interest rate changes

5) balance owed

6) minimum monthly payment

1) name of lender – If you have more than one account with the same lender then this could be Bank of X Visa™ or Bank of X MasterCard™.

2) last 4 digits of card number – for identification use only

3) Interest rate – I want to know which cards have the highest interest rate so that I know to pay these off first.

4) date interest rate changes – Many new credit cards come with an introductory

interest rate for the first X number of months. I want to know when this rate will change.

5) balance owed – Balance as of that date. I usually call the automated service of my lender to get an exact amount.

My Liabilities section may look like this;

Liabilities	Acct #	Interest	Until	Balance
Bank Y Car	1122	10.5%	12/5/2019	8,622.05
Bank X Visa	2211	12.99%	5/1/2016	1,201.00
Bank Z Visa	3344	18.99%	forever	2,000.00
Total debt				11,823.05

Total Assets and Liabilities(assets minus liabilities)= 871.95

This shows me what I am worth today, $ 871.95. But what else does it tell me? This document tells me who I should pay off first if I can afford it. Which bills you pay off first should depend on several facts.

The first thing to consider is whether you will need that money back if an emergency occurs. For example, you have an extra $ 100 a month in your budget and you would like to spend it to pay off your debt sooner rather than later. Great idea! But what will happen if your car needs repairs next month? Will you wish that you had not spent that money on paying down that bill? Do you have money saved up for such an emergency? If you have reasonably good credit, I would suggest you think of your credit card as your savings account. If you pay down the credit card (not store or gas cards) then you can use it to pay for the emergency while saving on the interest rate when there is no emergency. If your credit is bad then I would not take the risk that the lender will not close your credit card account. I would set up a savings account for emergencies before I pay any debt down (more than the minimum payment due).

Secondly, if you have plenty of excess money or are comfortable using your credit card as your emergency funds, then I would pay off the highest interest rates first. Benjamin Franklin is famous for having said "**a penny saved is a penny earned**". Saving money is actually more valuable than earning more money. Money earned is taxed, so a dollar earned may not be worth a dollar while a dollar saved is always worth the full dollar. If you are just starting out your credit profile **please remember our rules in Chapter 3**.

One of the ways that we keep our credit profile in good shape is to prepare for the unforeseen. Have either a savings account or available credit for the emergencies. Life happens to all of us, be ready.

Chapter 21: Think Like A Lender

If you think like a lender, you can see which habits and traits you need to develop in order to be considered a good credit risk. Thinking like a lender will help you understand how you must manage your money to be appealing to lenders. There are few tips that can put you into the right mind set:

Tip #52: Know how money works

Reading books about money and understanding how your accounts and loans work can go a long way towards helping you keep your credit in good repair. For example, if you know that some loans will charge you extra if you pay off your loan faster while others will not, you will be in a batter position to make financial decisions.

Plus, the more you know about money in general, the more comfortable you will feel with it and the better decisions you will be able to make, which will help improve your overall financial state and will help you keep your credit in good shape.

You don't need to do heavy-duty research to appreciate how money works. One easy way to consider money is to think of it the way you think of time. You likely hate to waste time and you want to make the best use of it possible. Apply the same attitudes to your financial life and watch your finances soar!

If overspending has caused you to have a bad credit score, consider the following sneaky mind set trick: equate your money with your time. For example, if you make twenty dollars an hour, then a magazine subscription of $20 will represent one hour of your work.

Imagine an hour of your work and ask yourself whether the subscription is worth the time you put into the twenty dollars. Once you start seeing money as something that comes from your hard work rather than a general "thing" impulse spending will seem much less attractive, and it will be easier to keep your credit card limits low and you bank account stocked up with cash!

Tip #53: Take care of those things besides a credit score that affect how lenders view you Lenders will often look at not only your credit score but at other financial indicators, such as your income, employment record, and savings. Keeping these things in order can complement your credit score and can help you get good overall credit. Some lenders have their own ways of calculating credit scores, so keeping your overall financial system in good shape is one way to ensure that you are in good shape in all lenders' eyes.

Be aware that when lender ask to see your credit score, the credit bureaus send not only your credit score, but also the top four reasons why your credit score is lowered. The most common reasons for lowered credit scores are:

1) Serious delinquency in repaying accounts or bills.

2) Public record of bankruptcy, civil judgment, or report to a collection agency

3) Recent unpaid or late paid debts or accounts

4) Short-term credit record

5) Lots of new accounts

6) Many accounts have late payments, defaults, or non-payments

7) Large debts or amounts owed.

Knowing that your lender sees these possible problems can help you see the need to develop the best possible face to present to a lender. Lenders who look at your entire credit report may get a more positive picture of you than lenders who see only a number and four reasons for a lower score.

Tip #54: Follow up on closed accounts You closed a store card years ago - but is it still listed as an open account? Bureaucratic mix-ups happen, often quite frequently. If you want to keep your credit score good, you need to follow up on financial details.

Whenever you close an account - whether it's a credit account, bank account, or utility company account, make sure that you get written confirmation that the account is closed and paid in full and then follow up a few months later with the company to confirm the closed account. This simple precaution can save you hours of frustration - not to mention a lowered credit score.

Tip #55: Don't move around a lot Lenders like to see stability - it suggests stability in financial matters as well as in your life, and makes you a better credit risk. Plus, every time you move, you may have to change your credit information - including switching banks. This actually negatively affects your credit score by not allowing you to develop long-term relationships with lenders.

Remember: Your current and past addresses are listed on your credit report even if they do not directly affect your credit score. Any lender looking at your full credit report will be pleased to see that you create a stable life for yourself. Not moving too frequently can also save you money on moving costs, which can add up quite quickly.

Tip #56: Don't change jobs frequently Of course, there will be times when you will have to change jobs. However, avoiding changing jobs unnecessarily will help improve your credit score by allowing you to stay in one place and build a steady financial situation.

Your credit report also shows your current and past jobs - if a lender sees that you change jobs frequently, he or she may wonder whether you have the life stability required to handle debt responsibilities. Also, the lender cannot see why you left a job. If there are many employers listed on your credit report, the lender may wonder whether you have not been fired from jobs and whether that is an indication that you will be unable to pay your debts due to unemployment at some point in the future.

A lender makes their money by the interest charged on a loan. If you default on a loan, you cause the lender to lose money. Above all, the lender wants to see evidence in your credit record that you have the traits that will make you repay the loan - with interest.

Frequent job changes may indicate - to some lenders - that you will simply disappear with the money or default on a loan. Having a stable life - including a longer-term job and one place of residence - may indicate to lenders, on the other hand, that you are building up roots in a place and so will be unlikely to move and default.

Tip #57: Avoid changing switching credit companies and credit accounts a lot Credit companies will often offer you special introductory rates, generous free gifts or other incentives to switch companies. However, you should resist the temptation unless you have a reasonable reason to switch. Establishing a good credit relationship with one company - having one credit card from your college days, for example - is a good way to show lenders that you are a steady sort of person who is likely to take money matters seriously. That is exactly what lenders want to see. Switching accounts and lenders makes you appear fickle and less than reliable.

Tip #58: Keep your records up to date Not knowing what is going on in your own financial life is courting disaster. Keep one file folder in your home which contains your financial information - and review this periodically. If something changes in your life - you get married, you start a family, you move or change jobs, look through your financial folder and contact everyone who needs to be contacted to update them on the change. This will help make sure that all your creditors have the information they need about you. Keeping your own records up to date will help you make sure that everyone who handles your finances is also up-to-date.

Tip #59: Always be sure that your creditors know your current address If you move and forget to inform all your creditors of your new address, you may not get all your bills, making you look like a deadbeat debtor and making your credit score plummet. Make sure that you either close your credit accounts or get your new address and contact information to your creditors.

When you move, make sure that you inform credit card companies, stores you have credit cards with, banks, credit unions, and anyone else you do financial business with. Better yet, also arrange with the post office to have your mail automatically forwarded to you at your new address. This will ensure that any creditors you may have overlooked will still be able to contact you - and you will have a second chance to remind them of your address change.

Tip #60: Talk to lenders and creditors Many people are hesitant to keep an open line of communication with their lenders because they are embarrassed about their financial state or because they feel unsure about the position.

Lenders can't read your mind, though. They do not know that you can't make a payment this month but will be able to make a double payment next month because of a banking error. They simply see that you have failed to make a payment - this may indicate a temporary problem or a decision on your part to default on your loan.

Without your input, your creditors have no way of knowing, and since their profits and money are at risk, they tend to take the more conservative view and even assume the worst. Keeping the lines of communication open as soon as a problem develops can help reassure your lenders and can help your creditors see that you are responsible with their money.

Talking to lenders as soon as a problem develops can be an effective way to prevent a ding on your credit score that can affect your credit score. For example, if you are giving trouble paying your bills, you can often work out a more reasonable payment schedule.

In most cases, you will not get a ding on your credit record if you do this because the lender will have some assurance that your financial obligations will still be met. In fact, one of the things that most credit repair companies do is to arrange for more reasonable payment schedules. With a simple phone call, you can do this for yourself for no charge.

Lenders want, above all, to be repaid so that their interest rates can earn them a profit. By communicating whenever there is a problem and showing that you are willing to work hard to meet your responsibilities, you show your creditors that they will get their money and this makes lenders more willing to work with you to ensure that your credit rating is not badly affected by one missed or late payment. Speaking with your creditors can help establish a good working relationship that can help keep your credit rating in good shape.

Tip #61: Get lenders to waive late fees and charges

If you have missed some payments or made some late payments, lenders will often charge you a fee for non-payment. This not only adds insult to injury - you have to pay more on your bills and get a ding on your credit - but also makes bills more difficult to repay since the bills are now higher. You can phone the lender and get the charge waived in most cases, though. This is a secret that credit repair companies have long known and is one of the first services they will perform on your behalf. You can easily accomplish this for yourself, however, at no cost.

Lenders want to get paid, and if they think that you will pay your bill more quickly by waiving the late fee, they will most often gladly remove the fee in exchange for prompt payment.

Develop an Organized Strategy to Repair Your Credit Score

Staying organized and on-track is very important when you are trying to boost your credit score, because there are so many details to follow up on and so many things to remember. A few basic organization tips can help make sure that you do not overlook anything that can cost you your good credit score:

Tip # 62: Stay financially organized Keep all your financial records - including tax records - in one place. Note the days you paid your bills on the bills themselves. Note how much you owe and where you owe money. Keeping your financial information in one place allows you to refer to it easily. Seeing all your financial life in one place also makes it easier for you to see where your credit and your financial life still needs work.

Some of the information you may want to keep in your financial file includes:

-Bills -Tax receipts and forms -Articles and pamphlets about debt -Your credit reports and scores -A list of contacts that affect your financial life (such as your bank and credit agencies, for example) -Your written emergency plan, detailing what you should do in case of a sudden loss of job or other problem -Banking information -Financial forms -Investment information -Deeds to your assets (such as your house) -

Agreements you have signed for loans and other financial services -A list of your financial goals -Insurance forms

You may want to buy a box and keep your separate information in different labeled folders (tax information together, for example, and bills in another folder) for easy referencing. Whatever system you use, you will find it much easier to manage your finances - and your credit - if you don't have to hunt for random pieces of paper.

Tip #63: Set short-term goals and do frequent credit self-checks in order to track your progress Credit repair takes time and effort. Some days, it will seem that you are getting no closer to a better credit score at all. In order to keep track of your progress and in order to keep going forward, you need to set goals and keep track of what you are doing.

For example, setting a goal such as "I will improve my credit score" is far too broad. Set smaller goals, such as "I will talk to my bank about budgeting this week" or "I will pay off half my credit card bill by next month." These goals work better because they are manageable and have a builtin deadline.

Writing your goals on a calendar or planner you look at everyday will motivate you to keep working on your credit repair and will keep you making the small steps that can lead to better credit. If you review how far you have come each month or week, you can really keep track of your progress and see how much you still have to do.

Tip #64: Take care of the details when applying for credit or for a credit report Little things make a big difference. Misquoting your social insurance number or using a slightly different name (Jane Doe Smith instead of Jane Smith) can make a big difference, since credit bureaus can count the two names as different people. Making sure that you fill out each financial form accurately and in the same way can go a long way in ensuring that there are no mistakes in identity that can affect your credit score.

Tip #65: Don't make the mistake of thinking that small differences in credit scores or loan interest rates won't make a big impact A few points on a credit score can mean the difference between a lender offering you a prime rate reserved for the best credit risks and the worse interest rate offered to less than prime customers.

This may amount to only a few percentages in different loan rates, but this can make a huge impact, especially on a large purchase. For example, a few percentage points on a longterm fixed-rate loan can mean the difference between tens of thousands of dollars saved - or tens of thousands of dollars overspent.

It is in your best interest to boost your credit score by every percentage point you can and to fight

for the very lowest interest rate loans you can. After all, if you have larger payments each month due to a higher interest rate than you deserve, it will be harder for you to repay your bills. Also, you will qualify for fewer loans if you have higher-than-needed interest rates, as you will be able to afford fewer of the larger monthly payments.

Tip#66: If you need to repair your credit, stay organized with a to-do list that ensures you won't forget anything

As you can likely tell by now, credit repair is not one magical solution but rather lots of relatively small things you can do to help repair your credit. To make sure that you don't over look any one thing, you may want to develop a to do list that you can post and check off.

You may list credit accounts you need to close, accounts you need to pay down, people you need to contact, and things you need to check out or research. As you tick off each item, you will get a real sense of accomplishment knowing that you are taking steps to improve your finances. Keeping a credit repair checklist posted will also keep you on track and let you know what you still need to do.

Tip #67: Automate your finances

Thanks to automatic bank payments, you can have your bills taken out of your checking account each month or even charged to your credit card. If you are the sort of person who gets dings on their credit report because you can never remember to pay your bills on time, this can be a very useful service.

You can even set up your email service to send you automatic reminders of bills that are due soon so that you can pay them. This sort of automation is one of the nicer things about high-tech living and can help you keep your credit score clean if your credit score suffers mainly from your own forgetfulness or disorganization.

Conclusion

Thank you again for purchasing this book!

I hope this book was able to help you be well on your way to establishing a good credit history for yourself! The information, techniques and advice presented in this book should motivate you towards fixing, maintaining, and growing your credit score far into the future and towards retirement. Being aware of why your credit is important and how you can maintain the health of your credit score can have vast and positive implications for your financial situation for years to come. Additionally, I hope that this book has provided you with the tips necessary to fix your credit if it's currently in shambles. Remember, take your credit score one financial transaction at a time. It's important to be responsible when you borrow money because there are consequences associated with being reckless.

The next step is to go out and implement the techniques presented in this book into your daily life. You are not going to be a credit guru overnight; it takes time to ground your habits in repetitious activity that over time will refine how you spend and borrow your money. When utilized correctly, the techniques presented in this book have the potential to revolutionize your credit score and your spending habits, but it's up to you to have the discipline and focus in order to see tangible results. It's most important to stay positive and not to get discouraged, especially if your current financial situation is less than stellar.